PRAISE |

"*Destinies* is a beautiful, touching and inspiring collection of true stories that will compel you to take stock of your life and move in the direction that your heart calls. You'll see that with the right tools and a willingness to move forward in life, you can achieve your dreams. If you need help in finding your destiny, this is the book for you."

– Marci Shimoff, #1 NY Times bestselling author, *Happy for No Reason, Chicken Soup for the Woman's Soul*

"*Destinies* is a well-written, thought provoking book that is written for those readers in search of finding their destiny. This book will help you define who you are today and show you how to move towards your destiny and achieve your goals. I truly enjoyed the book in its entirety. I highly recommend and encourage you to read it."

– Brian Proctor, VP of Business Development, Proctor Gallagher Institute

"*Destinies* is a powerful, inspiring and life-changing book that provides true stories of what's possible, for everyone, when you understand and implement the Law of Attraction. Highly recommended!"

– Arielle Ford, author, *The Soulmate Secret*

"You are one decision away from a completely different life." I love how this point is illustrated so clearly here. The desire for change and success + the decision to act, launched each writer into a completely different world. There were fears to plow through, choices to make, risks to take… but their dreams shone brighter than their doubts and they walked forward with faith. Allow *Destinies* to whisper deep into your soul as you ask yourself; What's my dream? Am I living it? What decision can I make today that will change my life forever? All it takes is one."

– Colleen Aynn, #1 International Bestselling Author, Professional Speaker Coach, www.colleenaynn.com

"It is never too late to take a new approach to change your destiny. As legal counsel to some of the writers, I have first-hand knowledge of their courage and vision that has them propelled through challenge and adversity, where others may be stopped. This book is a very powerful resource in helping you reach your goals and live the life worthy of who you are meant to be!"

– Banafsheh Akhlaghi, Esq., author of International Best Seller
Beautiful Reminders ~Anew, and entrepreneur.

"I am utterly in love with every person in this book. Each has shared from their heart in an authentic, vulnerable way that connects all of us as One. I know the readers will connect, too, and fall in love with not only the writers, but with that Oneness we all are all a part of."

– Rachel Bazzy, author

"If you're feeling stuck or yearning for a change, this book will change your life and way of thinking. It will leave you inspired and wanting more, the stories in this book will give you the boost that you need to make decision to take your life to the next level."

– Rosangela Vincenzo

PEGGY MCCOLL
BOB PROCTOR
SANDY GALLAGHER
and friends

DESTINIES

MOTIVATING STORIES
FROM ORDINARY PEOPLE
WHO CREATED
EXTRAORDINARY RESULTS

Published by
Hasmark Publishing, judy@hasmarkservices.com

Copyright © 2017
First Edition, 2017

Disclaimer

This book is designed to provide information and motivation to our readers. It is sold with the understanding that the publisher is not engaged to render any type of psychological, legal, or any other kind of professional advice. The content of each article is the sole expression and opinion of its author, and not necessarily that of the publisher. No warranties or guarantees are expressed or implied by the publisher's choice to include any of the content in this volume. Neither the publisher nor the individual author(s) shall be liable for any physical, psychological, emotional, financial, or commercial damages, including, but not limited to, special, incidental, consequential or other damages. Our views and rights are the same: You are responsible for your own choices, actions, and results.

Permission should be addressed in writing to destiniesbook@gmail.com

Editor, Erica Saunders
enickij@gmail.com

Cover and Book Design, Anne Karklins
annekarklins@gmail.com

ISBN-13: 978-1-988071-37-4
ISBN-10: 1988071372

 Hasmark
PUBLISHING

To You, The Reader

ACKNOWLEDGEMENTS

The idea for this book was inspired by an incredible man, Bob Proctor. Close to 40 years ago Bob inspired me to find my Destiny and pursue it, and I acknowledge him for choosing to do the same many years earlier. I am grateful for Bob Proctor. He has been my greatest teacher and is a cherished friend.

There is a positive ripple effect that occurs when people discover why they are here and what the purpose of their life is. Some call it their Destiny. And, many people in history have done just that; discovered their Destiny and shared it with others. As a result, many benefit.

The wonderful contributing authors who are in this book have given of themselves; their private stories, the pains from the past, their journey, their healing, their turning points and the results; as they share with you a story that can and will inspire you, if you let it.

I am grateful to every author who contributed to this book in such a giving, open, powerful, profound and positive way.

I am grateful for their teachers and mentors who inspired them.

I am grateful this collection is truly unique and has the potential to positively impact your life.

I am grateful for you, the reader, for choosing to invest in yourself and read this book.

I am grateful for those who share this book with others.

I am grateful for the blessed life that I live, appreciate and enjoy every single day.

I am grateful for Hasmark Services for bringing this book together in a way that is professional and available for you and millions of other readers.

Be sure to have fun discovering and living your Destiny, because life is meant to be fun.

To your Destiny,
Peggy McColl

TABLE OF CONTENTS

ACT IN FAITH

BY PEGGY MCCOLL

"Act as if it were impossible to fail."
– Dorothea Brande

At 19, the conditioning of my upbringing ruled me. I believed that everything that happened to me, up to that point in my life was caused by other people and circumstances beyond my control. I plowed through life angry and pessimistic, blaming others for my results. At the time, the company I worked for mandated all employees attend a personal development seminar. I was determined not to participate. After the threat of being fired for not attending, I begrudgingly arrived late to the session in protest. I had already made up my mind that this was going to be a complete waste of my time. Obviously, I wasn't in a mindset to grow. In fact, I didn't even know growth was a prerequisite to living a good life.

By the time I arrived, every seat in the auditorium was full except for an empty one in the front row. I sat down determined not to learn anything until I felt compelled to listen. The speaker had a commanding presence on stage and his message shook me to my core. My life changed forever when he quoted Vernon Howard and shared the following statement: "You can't escape from a prison if you don't know you're in one." My life was a prison – one of my own making.

The speaker, Bob Proctor, recommended three books, *Think and Grow Rich* by Napoleon Hill, *Psycho-Cybernetics* by Maxwell Maltz and *Your*

Erroneous Zones by Dr. Wayne Dyer. Immediately following the seminar, I rushed to buy these books, and not only did I read them, I devoured them. Every page was marked up, underlined and highlighted. I became a disciple of the study of personal development material in an effort to improve my position in life. I registered for additional seminars with Bob Proctor and immersed myself in the study.

For many years, I understood the material in theory, but I wasn't yet fully experiencing all the good I desired. With every new job, my workload responsibility grew and my salary increased, but I still wanted more. Eventually, I became fascinated (and quite frankly, frustrated) that the good I wanted in my life hadn't shown up yet. One day, while studying *The Science of Getting Rich* by Wallace D. Wattles something clicked. He said, "Through thought the good you desire comes to you, by action, you receive it." Bingo! The true meaning of the significance of what he was saying was obvious. In order to create and actually live the life of my dreams, I would have to act.

It was right around this time that my rocky marriage crash landed in divorce. I found myself a single woman raising a toddler. My desire was to own a home where my son and I could live, but I didn't have the money to buy one.

A friend told me about a special drawing where $100 would buy a raffle ticket for the chance to win a gorgeously designed, professionally decorated 'dream home'. I went to see the house, and fell in love with it. Right then and there in the foyer, I made a committed decision to own it. From all the studying over the years, I knew I had to first see myself in possession of it; I had to feel what it would feel like to own it, and I would need to take action to bring it into my life. So I bought a ticket and did the work of claiming it in my imagination.

Prior to the drawing for the dream home, I visited the house many times and with each visit tapped into my imagination all the while visualizing living in the house. The day of the drawing arrived but I didn't win. For a split second I was disappointed; however, I did not allow the disappointment to hijack the satisfying feeling of having a home. I stayed focused on living in a beautiful home, and wasn't attached to exactly which home it would ultimately be.

My life went on normally, taking my son to and from daycare, going to work, studying the material and feeling the feeling of owning my dream home. In the middle of the night a few weeks later, I was awoken by a booming voice that in a clear and firm manner said, "Go to the house!" I knew exactly what house the voice was talking about. The next morning I grabbed my winter coat, laced up my boots, and drove straight to dream house. To my amazement, there was a for sale sign in the front yard. The winner of the dream home had put the house up for sale. I realized in that moment, my vision of owning the house was coming true.

The next day, I called the real estate agent and asked to visit the house. As soon as I stepped through the door I could visualize my son and I making this our home. A few days passed and I decided to put an offer in, not knowing from where the money was going to come from. I had a job, a good job, but I didn't have the money for a down payment much less money to buy the house.

Going against everything that felt comfortable and the conditioning of my upbringing, I simply acted in faith that the money would show up when I'd need it. Here is where I learned the most valuable lesson of my life. It is a lesson that I have repeated time and time again as I've stretched myself far beyond what I ever previously thought was possible for me. The lesson is to combine believing and acting with DOING in faith.

Believing that you can have all that you desire is the first step. Acting as if you already have it is the second step. Doing is the third and final step. Unfortunately, leaving out any of these steps won't yield the results you desire.

Envisioning and feeling are acts of simply wishing and pretending without action. If you want the universe to give you what you want, you must act as if you already have it, but to receive it, you must DO. Action is the master key to manifestation. Sitting back and wishing for something won't make it happen. You must get off your rear end and do something. You must move yourself in the direction of your dreams.

The offer I made was 'unique' and included a significant down payment, an early move in date, occupancy fees paid for six months while I lived in the home, and a closing date six months after I moved in. The agent decided to present it to the seller, and gratefully, he accepted.

As the day of my move-in approached, the initial down payment, which was a significant amount, manifested from a retirement fund I created years earlier which until then I didn't think I could access. This provided the funds I needed to move into my dream home. Once I settled in, the next payment due for closing loomed on the horizon. Instead of worrying that I didn't have the money, I acted as if I did. I kept the faith believing the money would show up. It would've been easy for me to allow the fact that I didn't have the money to get in the way. Every time I thought about not having the money, I switched my thinking to the vision of owning the house with ease, and how happy my son and I would be making this house our home. Lo, and behold, just a few days prior to the scheduled money transfer, the company I worked for went public. Part of the benefit included purchasing stocks in the company at a reduced rate. When the Initial Public Offering (IPO) occurred, I generated all the funds I needed to close the deal. Like magic, right out of thin air it seemed to have dropped into my lap, but the truth is… this is how the universe works.

After studying this material and applying it to my life for more than three decades, it never ceases to amaze me what is possible. People don't get the results they desire for two reasons: either focusing on the lack of an idea or never acting on their idea. I'd like to take some time to discuss both issues that can doom a person despite their best intentions.

First, when something isn't showing up in your life, there is a tendency to focus on your conditions. As I was manifesting my dream home, it would have been easy for me to focus on the appearance of it not being mine. But the truth is all creation starts as a thought. Once someone imagines an idea of an outcome it can be manifested physically in the 'real' world. I first 'owned' the dream home and created the feeling of living in it despite the reality of my situation. By believing the house was mine I kept the dream alive. Instead of focusing on the fact that I didn't have the money or that I didn't win the drawing, I held fast to the feeling of owning my dream home and how happy my son and I were in the home.

Second, if you don't act on your idea, it probably won't magically appear on your doorstep one day. You must act. When I heard that booming compelling voice while comfortably slumbering in my bed, I knew I had to act. To this day I have no idea whose voice it was – maybe my subconscious mind or my guardian angel – who knows? The main point is that I heard the voice and I listened to it because it felt right. The moment I drove up to the house, I knew why I had listened. I was surprised, but at the same time not surprised at all, that the house was on the market. Staying true to my vision of owning that house, I kept the action going by calling a realtor.

The one thing I learned is having a scarcity mentality never serves anyone who wants to get ahead in life. The same can be said for not acting on a brilliant idea. Imagine if Orville and Wilbur Wright would've listened to their naysayers who told them they were crazy for trying to fly. We probably wouldn't be flying around in jumbo jets today. Thank goodness they ignored the naysayers and remained focus on acting on their vision.

The other thing required besides holding the vision of your desire is ACTION. Whatever you desire will come with seeming effortlessness if you move towards it.

A great analogy I often share with clients to illustrate this point is the metal shavings and a magnet on opposite sides of a table. Here, the power of the magnet isn't strong enough to attract the metal shavings. For the magnet to attract the shavings, it must move towards the metal shavings. As it does, the shavings begin flying in a massive rush towards the magnet. The same principle applies to goal achievement – once you have made a committed decision, your goal begins to move towards you. Don't allow yourself to become sad, depressed or quit when things don't seemingly come to you the way you think they should. There's a larger plan at hand to which you're not privy. Your only job is to hold fast to your vision, keep the faith every day, believe that it is already yours, and by law it will come to you.

Years ago, I became a true believer in the power of my mind when I manifested my vision of my first dream home. In doing so, following the process definitively proved to me how the universe works. It also showed me my role as a natural co-creator working in cooperation with the universe. Since then, I have stretched myself innumerable times to achieve bigger and better things. At every attempt, by holding fast to my vision, whatever idea I envisioned arrived right on time and always bigger and better than I could have ever hoped. Every time, I had feelings of doubt, worry and fear I am always able to quickly redirect my attention from conditions outside of me and turn my focus back to the marvelous vision of what I desire.

I have been studying this material for nearly 40 years. It works every time. If you don't believe me give it a try, but not half a try or a partial try, but an all-out, pedal to the metal all the way try until whatever it is that you desire has manifested itself.

You can have whatever your heart desires if you: use your imagination to envision the outcome of your dreams, have the courage to believe, and allow yourself to feel what it would be like to own your dreams. All of this can happen if you hold fast and do your part by taking action. Start small if you're so inclined to gain confidence in the process. Whatever you want can be yours. Living your destiny doesn't happen by accident. It happens when you decide. It happens when you feel as if you are already living the life. You will find that the process works every time – your only job is to be bold and take action to bring it about.

ABOUT PEGGY MCCOLL

Peggy McColl is a *New York Times* Best Selling Author. She is the Founder and President of Dynamic Destinies Inc. Her purpose in life is to "make a positive contribution to the lives of millions of others" and she accomplishes this via her books, audio programs, mentoring programs, teleclasses, speaking engagements and by helping authors spread their valuable messages throughout the world. She is also known as an Internet Marketing Expert and specializes in helping Authors and Experts build their brand, expand their business, experience revenue growth and create "best seller" status credibility. Her work has been endorsed by many, including: Bob Proctor, Debbie Ford, Marianne Williamson, Jack Canfield, Mark Victor Hansen, Neale Donald Walsch, Gregg Braden, and many others.

WHAT 50+ YEARS IN BUSINESS TAUGHT ME ABOUT DESTINY

By Bob Proctor

"Before you can do something you must first be something."
– Johann Wolfgang von Goethe

I strolled through the door not fully knowing what to expect. It was synchronistic that I was in the same city as the crew of the production company that was about to film me.

I hadn't prepared for the filming. In fact, I'd just heard of it a day or two before.

It was destiny for me to be in the movie *The Secret*. It was decades in the making, but it all came down to what I was about to do next.

You see, the "secret" literally changed my life about 55 years ago. I remember it like it was yesterday...

It started on October 21, 1961, when a man by the name of Raymond Stanford sat down with me. Raymond put an "R" on a sheet of paper with two "H's" and a "W" beside it.

Then, he looked at me and said, "Bob, let this 'R' represents results. The two 'H's represent happiness and health. The 'W' represents wealth. Do you think I'm a happy person?"

I said, "Yes, I think so."

Ray asked, "Have you ever seen me sick?"

I had to admit that I hadn't.

Then, he asked, "Have you ever seen me without any money?"

"No, I haven't."

Ray proceeded to tell me that he thought I was one of the most miserable people he had ever met.

He said, "You're never healthy, you always have a backache, or a cold or something. And you're always broke. Why don't you change this?"

I didn't really believe I could. I was making $4,000 a year, and I owed $6,000.

Ray said, "You can have anything you want. But you're going to have to change the way you're looking at your life."

"What do you mean?"

Ray responded, "You're looking at the fact that you never went to school, and you don't have any business experience. You're putting yourself down, and figuring out all the reasons you can't change.

"Your problem isn't a lack of education nor is it a lack of experience or money. You've got a perception problem. You're looking at yourself the wrong way. If you changed your point of view of YOU, your whole world would begin to change."

It was an invaluable lesson.

Today, the company that I own does millions of dollars in business. It operates in 47 different countries, and it's growing every day. And here I am 55 years later with a healthy body and very cheery disposition. And all I really did was change my point of view of who I was and what I was capable of.

Ray Stanford got me to read and study Napoleon Hill's *Think and Grow Rich*; it was the first book I had ever read. I read it every day, and my thinking – and my life – have never been the same.

I started a cleaning company and earned my first million within a few years. It was then that my calling first began to emerge.

You see, even though I was making my money from cleaning offices, I was really interested in helping the people that worked for me (and anyone else I came into contact with) change their thinking patterns and dream bigger.

I suppose I could have continued down the path I was on, reading every day, growing my cleaning business and bringing in more and more money. But one day I started wondering, *"How did my life improve so dramatically? What happened? What was the secret to my success"*?

I couldn't figure it out. After all, a whole bunch of people had read *Think and Grow Rich* and their lives hadn't changed. And I was taught that if you don't get a good formal education, you can't get a good job. Well, I had dropped out of high school, and I didn't have a good job – I owned the company!

I made up my mind that I was going to figure out what I had done that was allowing me to do so well.

It took me nine-and-a-half years of study before I was able to connect the dots. And that was it. I knew I wanted to spend the rest of my life teaching it to others.

One of the first things I did was write a book that encapsulated what I had learned over the past decade. I called it *You Were Born Rich*. I also started a coaching, training, and seminar company in the early 1970s.

I started traveling all over the world giving seminars, often speaking in front of thousands of people. And I kept creating bigger goals – I was on a mission to help as many people as possible break down paradigms and achieve success in all areas of life.

And that's when the call came…

It was the spring of 2006.

I worked with one of the men who appears in *The Secret*. He lives in Australia, which is where the film's production company is located.

Well, someone from the production company was talking with my client and mentioned that he had heard of me. So, my client gave him my cell phone number, and he also gave Rhonda Byrne, the Executive Producer, a copy of my book, *You Were Born Rich*.

Rhonda was on her way to the United States to shoot *The Secret*, and reportedly, my book was the only book that she took on the plane with her. She read it on her flight, and when she arrived in the States, she wanted me in the movie.

Rhonda's sister, Glenda was traveling with her, so she called me and left a message on my cell phone. Unfortunately, the message was garbled. I couldn't understand most of what she said. I saved the message, but I didn't think much of it.

Then, a few weeks later, I was talking with my Executive Assistant, Gina Hayden, and I remembered the message.

I said, *"Gina, I think this woman's name is Glenda, and I believe this is her phone number. Would you please call her to see what this is about? I think the message mentioned something about a film."*

When Gina called, Glenda explained that they were making the film and they really wanted me to be in it. Unfortunately, the crew was going back to Australia the next week. She said that they were shooting all weekend in Aspen, Colorado.

Gina said, *"Isn't that strange? Bob is doing a seminar this weekend in Aspen."*

It turned out that I was working right next door to where they were shooting. So I just walked in, sat down, and went to work.

The 90-minute film was released in the fall of 2006, and a half billion people have seen it. Now, if you watched the movie, you may remember that I was the first teacher to appear on the screen, and so now millions of people around the world recognize me as the guy from *The Secret*.

Filming that movie allowed me to reach more people in a few months than I had in 40 years. As a result, I was essentially an "overnight" success after decades of hard work and dedication.

Of course, it would not have happened if I hadn't put in all the work beforehand because that's what set everything in motion. It's what caused Glenda to call me in the first place.

To most people, the synchronicity of it all is uncanny, especially the part about me being in Aspen at the perfect time. However, I think differently than most people. I know that as I was moving toward my goal of helping more and more people around the world, the realization of that goal (*The Secret*) was moving toward me.

As I write this, I am 82 years old, and unlike when I was 26, I am happy, healthy, and wealthy. I am working all over the world and building wonderful relationships.

I still read every day, give people everything I've got, and I seldom play it safe. I encourage you to do each of those things to help you fulfill your destiny.

It is amazing how much more opportunity there is today. Because of technology, the world is much smaller now, and you can do things much faster. However, there will always be challenges when you try to fulfill your destiny. But if you hold on to the vision of what you want, keep stretching yourself, and you don't take no for an answer, then you will keep creating new ways to overcome those challenges and succeed.

And know this:

When you live your **destiny**, you can recapture the excitement of childhood. You're so happy and excited that you don't want to quit or retire. It drives you every day.

About Bob Proctor

In 1961, **Bob Proctor** started studying "Think and Grow Rich", and it transformed his life. In addition to studying the book, Bob listened to Earl Nightingale's condensed recording of the book thousands of times. Then, Bob worked shoulder-to-shoulder with Earl Nightingale at Nightingale-Conant from 1968 to 1973, before leaving to start his own personal development company. Today, Bob has studied thousands of books, continues to read "Think and Grow Rich" every day, and is considered the world's foremost expert on the human mind.

HIT SEND!

By Sandy Gallagher

> *"The only person you are destined to become
> is the person you decide to be."*
> – Ralph Waldo Emerson

My hands were sweating.

I was about to send an email to 2,000 of my clients and colleagues. The email was going to shock and disappoint a lot of them.

You see, the email explained that I was leaving my law practice. But I wasn't leaving to practice somewhere else. I was leaving to go into an entirely different industry. I wanted to help people achieve their dreams and create the life they truly wanted.

I had the email cued up and ready to go. All I had to do was hit 'Send.'

But I kept picturing my mom telling me, *"Ever since you were three years old, you've wanted to be a banking attorney, just like your dad. Your father is so proud of you. And your clients love you."*

I regularly handled billions of dollars in mergers and acquisitions and was an advisor to boards of Fortune 500 firms. And yet, I couldn't hit 'Send' on an email.

For me, it was always about doing and being my best. When you want to be your best, you do things that other people can't or won't. And I wanted to be the best banking attorney there was.

I got straight A's in school and when I graduated from law school, I received the AmJur award for graduating as the number 1 banking student in the country.

When I got out of school, I practiced on Wall Street with a very well-known firm for six years. We worked with large commercial and investment banks.

Then, I moved to the West Coast to practice with my father. We built a thriving community banking practice. And I became one of the top banking attorneys in the country.

Of course, I was making great money. I also had great friends, a beautiful house, horses, dogs … the whole nine yards.

But then, I started thinking, "*Is this all there is?*"

Around that time, a friend asked me to go to a three-day leadership seminar. I enjoyed that kind of thing, so I agreed to go.

On August 18, 2006, I headed to Vancouver, Washington, to attend the seminar. It was called *The Science of Getting Rich*, by Bob Proctor from the book *The Secret*.

The event started on a Friday night. I remember sitting there that first night. I can tell you what I was wearing and what Bob was wearing. I was mesmerized as I watched him on that stage. He was sharing fascinating information about how the mind really works, and how it controls our behaviors and our results. He explained so many things that I had never learned before.

I kept thinking, "*How the heck did I go through all of that education, get all of those degrees and spend all of that time in the business world and never hear any of this?*"

By the second day of the seminar, I started thinking, "*My gosh, if I could package this information and bring it into the companies and executives I've worked with over the past 20 years, what a difference it would make.*"

Before the day was over, I wrote in very tiny print in my workbook, "*I want to be in the inner circle of Bob Proctor's company. I want to be Bob's closest advisor, and I want to create a program with Bob to bring into the corporations that I have worked with.*"

Those three ideas really excited me, but I wrote them in tiny print because I didn't want anybody to see it. In fact, I slammed the workbook shut right after I finished writing.

Then all of the sudden, thoughts like these started popping up in my mind: *Who do you think you are? You're just an attorney. You don't know anything about producing programs and DVDs.*

And they just kept coming. My mind chattered away on all the reasons I couldn't do it.

But I kept listening to what Bob was teaching. And I started to see everything in a new way. For instance, Bob had this beautiful flag that said, "*You have Infinite Potential.*" Now I'd heard that many times before, we all have, but it never really meant anything to me.

But Bob got it to mean something on a very deep level. He got me to reevaluate who I was as a person and what is possible in this life. And I thought, "*You know what? We can do anything we want!*"

In just three days, I had learned the most important thing I had NEVER learned in school: how the mind works – and how it controls our behavior and whether or not we succeed.

I made an unequivocal decision before I left that room. I was going to do the three things I had written in my workbook –be in the inner circle of Bob's company, become his closest advisor, and create a program with him for corporations.

And I knew my life would never be the same.

When I returned to my home in Seattle, Washington, I began to immerse myself in the programs that Bob had created. Studying his material helped me understand that, even when I was a kid, I had been following what Bob was teaching.

I had always been different (or at least my results were) compared to most of the people I associated with or that I went to school with. And my friends were always trying to get me to conform, but I just couldn't do it.

For the first time, it was becoming clear to me why I was like I was. With respect to my personal goals, I was living in harmony with the laws of the universe. But if someone had asked me why I was doing well, I wouldn't have been able to explain it.

One day in late August 2006, the name of the program I wanted to create with Bob Proctor flowed into my mind – *Thinking Into Results*. I outlined the entire program, started creating it, and even started the graphic design.

All the while, Bob Proctor didn't know any of it.

Then, in June 2007, I was at a consultant training in Delray Beach, Florida, and I heard my name from behind.

"Sandy, are you free for lunch?"

I turned around, and it was Bob.

I couldn't believe it! I didn't know he even knew who I was.

"Are you free for lunch?" he repeated.

Of course, I was!

I'll never forget that meal. He ordered a grilled cheese sandwich with cottage cheese and tea with milk.

Even though I was thinking, *"Ew!,"* I ordered the same thing – and it was really good.

For a while, we had a very pleasant conversation. But then things got serious.

Bob said, *"I've heard what you want to do. I've looked into your background, and I've decided we're going to go ahead and do this. And here's the deal...*

"You're going to own 25 percent of this company. The company is going to be called Life Success Corporate. You're going to do all the work, including doing all the production, and you're going to pay all the production costs. And it's going to cost you $500,000. You don't have to answer right now."

I sat there trying not to choke on my cottage cheese and pretended like everything was cool.

That evening, I did not talk to anybody – not any of my colleagues or anyone in my family. I just sat there and reflected.

I thought, "*You know what? This is what I had in my mind; this is what I wanted.*"

But I had to dig deep and answer the question: Am I willing to do what it takes?

I did not have $500,000 sitting in the bank in liquid assets. I had investments, but they were all locked up. And of course, there were many things I had to consider.

By midnight, I had decided I was going to do it.

I went to a seminar the next morning. There were 683 participants. We were in a big long, room and it was kind of dark.

Bob walked out on stage. With bright lights in his eyes, he announced, "*Our company's growing and we've attracted a lawyer!*"

Now, we hadn't signed any agreements. I hadn't even said yes. Nothing.

Yet, there he was saying, "*We've attracted this lawyer*" and he looked out in the audience and pointed me out.

Then, he said, "*We do have a deal, don't we?*"

I nodded my head, and he said, "*Ah, she nodded her head yes – we have a deal!*"

For the next year and a half, I continued to work on the Thinking Into Results program, and I helped out with Bob's 19 companies.

In December of 2008, I sat down with Bob, and I told him about some issues that he needed to address, or he was going to run into real trouble with his business.

He said, "*Well, do you know how to fix it?*"

"*Yeah, I know how to fix it.*"

"*Will you come in and run the companies?*"

19 companies, and I was still practicing law full time.

I said, *"Okay, on one condition; you've got to back me 100 percent. I'm going to do things you don't want, and I've got to do it to get this ship turned around."*

He agreed and January 14, 2009, I started as CEO.

In April of 2009, I was still practicing law, running 19 companies, finishing up *Thinking Into Results* and running the law practice.

Bob walked in, looked at me and asked, *"What are you doing?"*

I wanted to tell him that I was fine, and I could do it all, but he was looking at me with "that look."

Then, he said: *"Are you in or are you out?"*

I had really deluded myself that I could do it all. But now it was decision time.

So, that's when I was sitting there with the email I told you about. I was terrified to send it. Being a lawyer was all I had ever wanted to be.

I couldn't do it, so I picked up the phone, and I called Bob. I said, *"Bob, I can't – I just can't."*

"Hit Send – jump! You'll develop wings along the way: hit send!"

And wham, I did it! It was like I heard the email go "swish" as it went out.

I went to the outbox, hoping beyond hope that it had gotten hung up. It hadn't. It had gone to 2,000 people. Oh my God!

Within 24 hours, I received 892 replies. My amazing clients and colleagues wrote things like:

"I wish I had that kind of excitement about something."

"I wish I felt I was living my purpose."

"I wish I had that kind of courage."

There were even three people who said, *"I would love to do something like that, but I'm going to sit here until the day I die."*

I had written that email four and a half months earlier. I spent a lot of time writing it. It explained why I was changing careers. I talked about how much I really cared about the new industry. It was an excellent letter.

But, I just couldn't get to the point of sending it out. I kept thinking about the fact that I was an equity partner in a large law firm. That's like being a tenured professor; they can't fire you. It's a very stable position. And then there were the clients that I built up over 20 years.

Not only that, I was going into this new world that was so different. I wanted it so badly, but my conditioning kept telling me to wait. It was trying to rationalize, trying to reason and talk me out of it.

However, as I look back, sending that email was the most liberating moment in my life. It allowed me to live my **destiny** fully.

The key to success boils down to controlling your own destiny and not being at the mercy of others. Set goals that excite you and develop a burning desire for them.

Each time you set a goal, hold the vision of having already achieved it. Engage all five of your senses as you picture and feel the goal as already in existence. That has become the story of my life.

And remember, when the time comes to jump, don't retreat to what you've always known. Hit send – and you'll develop wings along the way!

About Sandy Gallagher

In 2006, a very successful attorney named **Sandy Gallagher** attended one of Bob Proctor's three-day seminars. Those three days transformed her life and eventually she joined forces with Bob to create the Proctor Gallagher Institute.

THE GIFT OF GIVING:
WHY I HAVE BEEN CALLED TO SERVE
THE STORY OF AN UNSTOPPABLE WOMAN!

BY CYNTHIA KERSEY

Who knew that when my husband of 20 years and I separated in December 1999, my pain would open the door to my greatest purpose.

Prior to our separation, we planned on spending the holidays with my parents in Florida. How quickly that went from being a family trip to one where my son and I would travel alone. Feeling devastated and overwhelmed, I promised myself that the next Christmas would not find me at my parents' house feeling sorry for myself. Instead, I would dedicate myself to a greater purpose – doing something for someone else.

As soon as I returned home, I called my mentor and friend Millard Fuller, the founder of Habitat for Humanity International, and asked him for advice. We first met each other when I interviewed him for my first book, *Unstoppable*. To this day, I remember what he told me when I confided in him about my separation. He said, "Cynthia, when you have a great pain in your life, you need a greater purpose." He went on to share with me about his recent visit to Nepal, one of the poorest nations in the world, and suggested that building a house for a Nepalese family in need could be a great project for me.

As I pondered his suggestion, I thought, "How many houses would I need to build that would be bigger than this pain?" Even though I had never built a house, it wasn't until I got to the number '100 houses' that it felt bigger than my pain.

I would be the first to tell you this was a crazy audacious goal which I had *no idea* how I would make it happen! I was a single mom, living off the sales of my $14.95 book and each house would cost $2,000. I had no big community of potential donors to draw from and didn't even know in what part of the world Nepal was located! This did not stop me because I had a purpose bigger than my pain and was invigorated by my new project. I was also grateful to have something to take my mind off my problems.

Throughout that year while grieving the loss of my marriage, there were times when I felt so terribly trapped by the walls of depression that I didn't even want to get out of bed. It was in those moments, I'd think about the Nepalese families who didn't even have a decent place to sleep at night. Reminding myself of my purpose energized me in those despondent moments to get up and move forward.

One year after my separation and a subsequent phone call to Millard, I achieved my goal of raising $200,000. I remembered, after committing to the goal, how impossible it seemed at the time. Who would have thought that by simply asking everyone I met to donate, I would achieve this goal? The money raised allowed me to assemble a team of 18 volunteers that accompanied me to Nepal over the New Year's holiday. What happened next was incredible – we built the first three of the 100 houses that would subsequently be built over the following year.

I'll never forget the connection I formed with a woman who received one of the homes we built. Chandra was also a single woman supporting several family members including her parents, brothers and sisters that lived with her in her tiny one-bedroom shack.

Although Chandra worked and diligently saved money each week for almost 18 years while working at a biscuit factory, she would never be able to save enough money to build a home without the help of our project. Her gratitude was apparent in her constant smile. Even though we didn't speak the same language, our hearts connected. When it was time for me to leave we were both in tears, she begged me to never forget her. As we hugged and said our goodbyes I thought, "Forget you? How could I ever forget you? You were the purpose that got me through the most difficult year of my life!"

When I started this project, I thought I was doing something great for these families. What I didn't expect was how this project would change my life forever! This was the first time I really experienced the transformational power of giving.

I also experienced something else firsthand – the Law of Giving and Receiving. Unexpectedly, that year I earned more money speaking and selling my $14.95 book, than I had earned in a very successful corporate sales career earning a six-figure income. It was as if a veil had been lifted allowing me to understand the spiritual axiom, "Give, and it shall be given unto you." The Scripture doesn't say wait until you GET something, whether it's getting more money, more time, more love, more support, or more resources. It says GIVE.

What transpired during my time in Nepal made something very clear to me: the law of receiving is activated by giving. When we wait for something in the future to change before we give, it puts us in a congested state. Stopping the circulation of giving is like stopping the flow of blood – our cells begin to die and our body ceases to function. The same can be said when we wait to give, a channel through which the universe can work is cut off. Understanding this principle fundamentally impacted how I ran my business. With every new book or project I launched, I attached a philanthropic project to it. This ignited a deep passion in my heart and brought great joy and meaning to my business, and even more so my life.

When my 2nd book *Unstoppable Women* came out in 2005, I was looking for my next philanthropic project. Unexpectedly, I received an invitation to attend the first ever Rural African Women's Conference. The only information I had was that women from rural Kenya were going to meet with us and share their story. Although my schedule was fully booked, I knew I had to say yes. Without knowing what to expect I booked my flight which flew me half way around the world.

There were forty other women from North America who also said yes and we all flew to the Nairobi airport for the next step of our journey. Picture this, it's hot and muggy; I am crammed on a crowded uncomfortable bus with women I didn't know ten minutes ago. What's worse, the shock absorbers are definitely not working. It's been 12 long exhaustive hours and with each bump in the road, I felt more and more uncomfortable while getting crankier by the minute.

I had a moment when I thought, "God please help me get over my little self so that I don't miss why I was called to fly half way around the world."

An hour later, we drove around a corner where I could see our destination in the distance. It was a very modest college campus where the women's conference was to be held. As we got closer, I could see what appeared to be a couple hundred women standing in the driveway smiling and waving. I thought, "Wow, they must be here for us!"

As I exit the bus, a woman took my hand and pulled me into the middle of this large group of women, we all began singing and dancing. In that moment, the last 12 hours disappeared – I was in heaven!

The next morning at 8:00 a.m. I walked into an auditorium filled with 400 women waiting to take the stage. I found out later that although many of the women had never left their small village before in their life, it did not stop them from walking for miles, many of them days, to meet with me and the 40 other mzungas (white people).

Over the next five days, each woman stood up and through an interpreter told their heart wrenching story. The first woman shared how her youngest daughter contracted malaria and the nearest medical clinic was 20 miles away. She carried her daughter for a full day and before she reached the clinic, her daughter died in her arms. What made her death even more heart breaking, is that she could have been saved with medicine costing about $3, the price of a cup of coffee.

The next woman told us that she and her eight-year old daughter spend 4-6 hours every day fetching water and firewood to keep their family alive. That didn't leave them any time to do more productive things like attend school or allow her to earn an income to adequately care for her family.

The third woman told us that her family frequently goes without food for days because they have no way to preserve fruits and vegetables. It's even worse in times of drought.

As I listened to their stories, it didn't come as a surprise to me that their greatest hope and concern was, "How can we get our children an education? Without it, nothing will ever change." These women weren't here to complain. They were looking for practical solutions to create a better life for their children and their families.

As I listened attentively and observed the faces of these women, I felt great empathy and sadness for things they had to endure. I could not imagine myself or my child living in such harsh conditions. But after hearing one heartbreaking story after another, my empathy turned to outrage. It didn't seem right that simply by virtue of where they were born, they'd live a life of back-breaking poverty, with little way out.

A voice in my head as clear as the ringing of a bell said, "Cynthia, you've got to do something about this!" Immediately, I heard an even louder voice that said, "This problem is so big and has been going on for too long. What difference could you really make?" Feeling overwhelmed, I decided to ignore both voices and be present to the experience I was having.

Five days later, it was time to get back on the bus. While saying my goodbye's, and hugging these women I had since fallen in love with, their faces and their voices pleaded with me about something I couldn't understand. I turned to my interpreter and asked "What are they saying?" He replied "Please don't forget us." Instantly, something welled up inside of me and I couldn't ignore their pleas. I promised these women, who I considered friends, that I would do something to help them.

Unlike my thoughts during the 12-hour bus ride to the college campus, my mind during the return trip focused on one thing – how to find an answer to the question, "What am I going to do about this?… Cynthia, you made this promise, where do I even start?"

During a visit to my friend Debbie Ford's over Thanksgiving she shared with me how her son Beau did the most wonderful thing for his bar mitzvah. Instead of getting a bunch of gifts or cash, he wanted to do something meaningful by asking people to donate money to build a school in Uganda.

When I heard this, it was as if a light bulb came on. I knew in that moment, what I needed to do to make good on the promise to my friends – the women of Kenya. I was going to turn my 50th birthday, which was coming up soon, into something meaningful by having a party and turning it into a fundraiser. I wanted to build a school in East Africa like Beau had done.

We booked the Shanghai Reds Restaurant in Marina Del Rey, California and I invited all my friends to attend. Instead of giving me a gift, I asked them if they could help me give children in East Africa a present – the gift of an education. That night 100 people attended, it was standing room only. Something else happened that I didn't anticipate – people were coming up and thanking me! It wasn't the typical "thank you for having a great party." They were thanking me for giving them the opportunity to make a difference – to be able to contribute to something that would forever change the lives of hundreds of children around the world. That night we raised $80,000. I thought, if I could do this in one night, imagine if I really put my time and energy into it.

It was clear to me what I needed to do to keep my promise to these women in a bigger way. I decided to get serious and open the Unstoppable Foundation. While doing some research I **discovered something that shocked me**.

Too many schools built by well-intended organizations in developing countries were sitting empty. Why were they empty? I learned that you can build a school... but without access to clean water, girls spend hours every day fetching water and aren't able to attend school.

You can build a school... but if children don't have access to basic medical treatment, they're often too sick and unable to attend.

You can build a school... but if children don't have nutritious food, they're hungry and malnourished.

You can build a school... but if the parents can't generate an income, the well-intentioned project can't sustain itself.

I had an epiphany. If this is going to work, we would need more than a school. We would also need to provide the kids with access to: clean water, healthcare, nutritious food, and training for the parents to earn an income so the entire project can be self-sustaining.

This became my marching orders as I searched for an organization to help me implement all five pillars. I was fortunate to find a partner on the ground in Kenya. *We Charities* had the expertise and experience in implementing all five services. The partnership between the Unstoppable Foundation and *We Charities* led to the creation of a program called Sponsor a Village.

It's not charity in the traditional sense – it's empowerment!

After creating the Sponsor a Village program, I began asking people to join me in this vision. What I discovered is that people really care. They care about others… whether they're in their own communities or half way around the world. They didn't only give but they asked their friends to write checks. They 'gave up' their birthday parties and replaced it with fundraisers, even their children had fundraisers.

The results have been both incredible and amazing. With the help of our generous supporters, we have educated over 30,000 children and impacted over 50,000 men, women and children in the Maasai Mara alone. We have expanded our five-pillar Sponsor a Village model to India. Entire communities are now thriving with the tools to lift themselves out of poverty.

Never would I have imagined that the choice I made in 1999 to find a purpose bigger than my pain would have been the doorway to a whole new life that would shape my **destiny** forever. It has brought me indescribable joy, meaning and satisfaction. The joy of working with friends like Bob Proctor, Sandy Gallagher, Peggy McColl and other generous supporters on this mission is the greatest gift of all.

As my mentor, Millard Fuller always said, "I feel like the richest person on the planet."

To learn how you can be a part of this important mission, go to UnstoppableFoundation.org for more info.

ABOUT CYNTHIA

Cynthia Kersey is the founder and CEO of the Unstoppable® Foundation. She is a respected leader in the transformational industry, a best-selling author of two books, "Unstoppable" and "Unstoppable Women" and an international speaker. Cynthia embodies her message and has integrated giving and contribution into her life and business for well over two decades. The Unstoppable Foundation is providing a daily education to over 10,128 children, and provides access to life-saving services such as clean water, health care and nutritious food through organic gardens to over 50,000 men, women and children in Kenya alone!

CAN DREAMS REALLY COME TRUE?

BY MICK PETERSEN

The flames from the 50 candles on my birthday cake shot up high enough to catch the house on fire. *Am I really 50 years old?* I asked myself while my family sang Happy Birthday. For a moment I got scared that time would run out before I could do everything I wanted to do in my life. *NO! There's still time* I told myself. If Ray Kroc could build his MacDonald's empire after 50, or if Julia Child could publish her first cookbook after passing the half century mark, or if Betty White could catch her big break on *The Mary Tyler Show* after her 50th birthday, or if Charles Darwin could change the scientific community forever with his first book, *On The Origin Of Species*, when he was 50 years of age, then I could make my dream true too. As I blew out the last candle, the decision was made – I would create my global franchise based on my best-selling novel *Stella and the Timekeepers* with a renewed, laser-focused precision.

The inspiring stories of the aforementioned trailblazers prove that no one is ever too old to live their dream. If they could do it, so could I. Like me, the accomplishments of their younger selves gave no indication they would live extraordinary lives later in life. Nothing happened for them until they made the decision to risk it all, and create their own destinies.

For me, it all started with a dream…

When my life was at its lowest point, I was shocked out of a depression by an extraordinary and otherworldly dream. In fact, it was so exceptional that for the next few years as I reassembled the shards of my shattered "real" life, my mind constantly returned to further explore that beautiful, and exciting imaginary world. It became a personal sanctuary during troubled times.

One day I realized that I should share it with others by writing it down in a book, *but where would I start?* During a dinner conversation in October of 2011, I told a friend about the dream and my book idea.

"You should sign up for National Novel Writing Month affectionately called NaNoWriMo," he said.

As soon as I got home, I googled National Novel Writing Month and discovered it was an online event during the month of November. New writers and seasoned professionals sign up for the event to motivate them to write 50,000 words of their manuscript. Within minutes, my imagination raced with possibilities. I knew I could do it if I put my mind to it. *I'm going for it* I decided.

For the next month, my daily goal was to add at least 1,666 words to my story. Every day before disappearing into my work, I would say to my partner, "I'm the next JK Rowling and my work is the next Harry Potter." At first, he rolled his eyes, dismissing me as a lunatic, but I didn't care because when I got lost in the world of my characters, in my mind, I became the male version of JK Rowling. By day 10, he started to believe it too. My new vocation consumed me.

With every passing day, my belief grew and it was here that I accidentally learned my first lesson in goal achievement – acting as if it already was. It felt a little bit phony at first, but with repetition you just start believing it. Later, one of my mentors told me, "Before you can **have** something, you must first **become** what you desire."

By the end of the month I had put the finishing touches on the first draft, my manuscript consisted of 68,000 words. I had done it, but now what? I had no idea what to do with it next. The book I had dreamt about writing, sat untouched for 3 years on my computer, almost long enough for me to forget about it – **almost**.

My life continued much as it had before the book. I worked as a Flight Attendant and managed my rental properties, but I wanted more. One day I asked myself *Is this all that life has in store for me?* I was ready for a change.

When I told a friend I wanted more out of my life, she said, "If you want something different, you have to make room for it to come in." I knew she was right. At that moment, I decided to sell all my rental property to create the space for something different.

The day my largest multi-family property sold, I remember sitting in my truck at the bank after depositing the check feeling buoyant and free.

A space had opened in my life for the good I desired. When I checked my email on my phone, I opened a 15-minute Bob Proctor video that changed my life forever. His message was about how I could have the life of my dreams and I was destined to do bigger and better things; I deserved the best life had to offer, and that it was all in the way I was thinking. When the video ended, I bought VIP tickets to an upcoming seminar he was conducting in Dallas, a mere four hour drive from my home in Galveston, Texas. It wasn't clear why I felt so compelled to attend the event, but, for some strange reason, I was looking forward to it. I *knew* I had to be there.

On the first night of the seminar, Bob said, "There is a science to getting rich, and specific universal laws were put in place that if followed could help everyone have a healthy, wealthy and happy life." It wasn't clear to me at the time what he was talking about, but I knew I had to pay attention. *You don't have to do certain things, rather you need to do things in a certain way.* Later that night, when we got to the hotel room, I kept asking myself, "Why haven't I ever heard any of this information before?" How much easier would my life have been if I would've lived according to these principles all along?

The next morning, the seminar participants waited for the main auditorium doors to open. In the middle of the room, and out of the corner of my eye, I noticed a woman. She noticed me too, and trained her eyes on me. Like a hawk eying its prey, she swooped in and introduced herself. After a brief conversation about a necklace she was wearing that her daughter had given her, I asked her what she did for a living.

"Oh," she said confidently, "you don't know who I am?"

"No," I said, thinking this woman must be full of herself with a comment like that.

"I didn't mean it that way!" she apologized. "My name is Jennifer Colford, and I thought perhaps you remembered when Bob introduced me last night. I am an International Best-selling Author."

At that point, I withdrew from the conversation, retreating inward. Perhaps the reason for attending the event was to meet her and talk to her about my book. When I told her, she wanted to hear all about it. Before I could finish telling her the concept, she grabbed my arm and said, "Come with me, there's someone I want you to meet."

In the center of the main auditorium stood a woman surrounded by a dozen people who hung on her every word. Jennifer pushed her way through, blurting out, "Peggy, you have to hear about this guy's book. It's amazing!"

"My name is Peggy McColl. I help authors make their books best-sellers."

We became fast friends. In fact, she introduced me to her sister who invited me to submit a story for an upcoming book she was launching called, *Unwavering Strength volume two*.

After lunch, Bob invited Peggy on stage to share with the audience about her business. She announced an upcoming online class she'd be teaching over the next six months. I knew I had to sign up for it.

The time flew by, and by the end of the weekend, we had learned a tremendous amount of information and planned to continue training with Bob in a year-long mentoring program.

Weeks later, I began the class with Peggy and the coaching with Bob. I dove headfirst into both of them and believed everything they taught with an unwavering conviction. *If these people are millionaires, doing what they love then I want to be like them*, I told myself.

In short order, I was working with a publisher, an editor, a graphic designer, taking courses on web design and doing many things I had never before contemplated. I marveled at myself. During the process, Bob and Peggy both encouraged me. I got the feeling they genuinely believed in my success wholeheartedly. So did Jennifer who persisted in her request to read my manuscript. "It's not ready yet," I said, "there's still too much work to be done on it." Eventually she said, "Just let me read it! Someday you'll release the book and PEOPLE ARE GOING TO READ IT!"

I finally agreed on the condition that her constructive feedback be delivered with kindness. After reading it, her response was, "Holy cow! How did you think all that up? It's amazing. I believe you have written the next Harry Potter." This was quite a confidence booster, giving me the encouragement to carry on.

Over the summer, I committed to an April 28, 2015 book launch. Through the fall and winter, I worked diligently and enthusiastically toward my launch. The last thing I did the night before my book was to be released was send a short email to Phillip Goldfine, Oscar and Emmy winning Hollywood producer whom I had met at a seminar the previous November. "Great," he said, "send me the electronic version and I'll take a look."

Finally, my April 28th launch day arrived. All the components of Peggy's teachings were in place and ready to go. *If this doesn't work, it's not from my lack of trying* I thought.

My book was a #1 best-seller on Amazon that day. As that sunk in, emails poured in from readers – mothers, daughters, sons and fathers, everyone raved about the book and seemed genuinely excited about the story. On the heels of this exciting news, Phil the producer, called to tell me he loved the book.

"Want to make it into a movie?" he asked.

"Sure!"

"When can you come out to Hollywood?"

"I am available anytime."

We arranged a meeting in Los Angeles at Universal Studios on July 9, 2015. Phil's objective to meet with me wasn't clear, but instead of getting caught up in worry, doubt and fear, I followed the next principle of goal achievement – hold to your vision no matter what the outside world may show. So I did.

Kevin, Peggy and Denis made the trip with me. After showing our identification, we received visitor's passes and we drove past administration buildings, sound stages, and movie trailers. We drove past Bob Zemeckis' parking spot and Stephen Spielberg's production company. We were really in the heart of Hollywood!

We parked in front of Phil's bungalow, and he bounded out to greet us. In his office, his magnificent Oscar glowed gold on his desk. After some small talk, he told my entourage I'd text them when we were done then Phil and I headed to the executive dining room.

The maître d' kindly welcomed us at the podium with a smile. "Right this way, Mr. Goldfine," she said, leading us to a corner table in the front atrium. We ordered our food and continued telling jokes and stories until finally Phil said, "Let me tell you the deal."

This was my first negotiation with a Hollywood type, and my belief told me to keep my guard up or I'd get screwed. *We'll see about your offer* I thought to myself.

"I had my creative director read your book. After he finished it, he sent me an email, telling me to read it too. He told me it was a four quadrant project."

"What's that?" I asked, feeling a bit stupid, but hey this was all new to me.

"It's the holy grail of movie making. Each quadrant represents a demographic – men, women, boys and girls."

"So that's good?"

"Yes! Welcome to Hollywood royalty. I'm going to make you the next JK Rowling," he said. My eyes must have been the size of dinner plates because he quickly reassured me, "Don't worry. It takes a long time to bring a project of this size to fruition, but just know I think your book series, once developed, could become a big franchise including theme park rides. I have all the awards, but not a ride. Stella will have a ride."

The surreal afternoon continued with a guided tour of the Universal back lot, a visit to the Universal theme park for a ride on a new 3D experience and a couple of selfies on movie sets on the back lot. We returned to his office to discuss the contract.

"Do you have representation?" Phil asked.

"I have a literary agent."

"You're going to need a lot more than that," he said. "You'll need an entertainment attorney, a publicist, a marketing strategist, an accountant among other things. Essentially, you'll need a team of experts to represent you as we create this franchise, but as I stated before, this will take quite some time, so you won't need them all in place right away."

When I texted my friends to pick me up, they came back to Phil's office where he shared his vision for the Stella franchise. They were just as shocked as I had been by the size and scope of the goal.

After we signed the contract, Phil offered me the use of an office in his bungalow at Universal Studios if I needed a place to write. At this point, I decided to reengage with my literary agent.

While I was reading Chapter 3 on Decision in *Think and Grow Rich*, Napoleon Hill's masterpiece, I came across a passage taken from the Bible. It was a verse from Matthew 18:19 that reads "And further I say to you that if two of you agree on earth concerning anything that you ask, it will be given to you by My Father in heaven."

In preparing for my meeting with my literary agent, Johanna Maaghul, I decided since Phil and I had already agreed to bring the Stella franchise to the world, it was already done. My goal in setting the meeting was to come from the place in which the goal was already done and to see if she was the right agent for me. When I mentioned the Bible verse, she recited it by heart. She understood where I was coming from and jumped right in and got to work.

I wrote my book, made it a best-seller, and got the film rights optioned all as a self-published author. It was time to go big-time and get a publisher involved, someone who believed in what we were all trying to accomplish, and would roll up their sleeves and get to work.

"I think you should rewrite your book with the help of a world-class editor, and I know just the right person for the job," Johanna said. "But he is very selective with whom he works. Chances are pretty high that he will say no, but it's worth a shot."

An email introduction brought David Ord and me together, and we scheduled a call. He said before reading any of my work, he wanted to hear my voice, look into my spirit and understand the intentions I had for my book. Our phone call lasted nearly two hours. At the end of the call he said he was enthusiastic to read my book now that he got a chance to talk with me. He had explained that two of the authors he had worked with were both guests on Oprah multiple times and each had sold millions of books.

Two weeks later while working at Phil's bungalow, Johanna informed me that David was excited to work with me. "He wants to set up a conference call with us later today."

The call was set for 5:15 pm pacific time. At 5:00 pm, Phil came in and said, "Hey, let's go see the new Star Trek movie."

"I can't," I said, "I have a call at 5:15."

"Come on, let's just go. You can step out of the theater to take the call. I have a meeting with the director tomorrow and I want to see his latest work."

Was I dreaming this? Here I was, writing in Hollywood, going to see a movie with an Oscar winning producer who was meeting with the director of the latest Star Trek movie? How did this happen?

We piled into his Aston-Martin DB9, put the top down and drove to the theater. On the way, with the wind blowing through my hair, I felt as if I had arrived. My goal to work in Hollywood had manifested.

At the movie theater, I stepped into the hallway to take the call, and to hear David's praise of my work and his vision to improve it. Further instructions on how to proceed would be forth coming. But the fact that I had an executive editor with whom I was to begin working got me very excited. My dream, our dream was coming into view.

Over the next few weeks, David and I collaborated on rewriting the first six chapters of the book with marked improvements to the prose, character development and sense of place. When we were both happy with the result, we turned our attention to improving my book proposal. Originally, I had framed it to show all of the accomplishment thus far with the book as a sort of beta-test whose results were phenomenal. With David's help, we shortened it and made it more compelling for the potential editors at big publishing houses.

In the beginning of August, I sent the all-new book proposal to Johanna, who said it was fantastic and she couldn't wait to send it out on September 1st.

"What!" I fussed. "No, you have to send it out immediately."

"Trust me," she reassured, "I have a strategy for that date. It's the new moon and all the 'big' book deals happen in the fall."

As hard as it was, I agreed, but I still wasn't sure if this was correct. I asked David about it. He said, "Absolutely. September 1st is not only a New Moon, but it's also a double eclipse which will magnetize its energetic force tenfold." Still not convinced, I did a google search and stumbled across a site that stated the following: Just know that Eclipse Seasons accelerate the process of change and transformation in the world and in your personal life. We have entered a big new chapter or season of our lives. The transition time has been from the spring of 2014 to now. Look back at your life prior to spring of 2014 and look at it now." I froze when I read this because I realized how this whole process with Bob Proctor and Peggy McColl helping me realize my dream with publishing my book had begun.

Johanna further surprised me when she negotiated a deal with David to work with me on a percentage basis, the first he had ever done in his illustrious career as a writer and an editor. Since I could hardly afford to pay him his going rate for his services, this seemed like a win-win for both of us. He said, "I am not a gambling man, but I feel like your book is worth the risk. We either make nothing or we change our lives and have the opportunity to work together on many more books."

In my pocket, I carry around a tattered card encased in a plastic sleeve with my goal written on it. Behind it, I have placed a folded check for $5,500,000. Oftentimes, I remove the card, think about how I would feel with my goal fulfilled. I also remove the check and examine it, relaxing into a state of what it would feel like once I had manifested my dream. Over and over on a daily basis, I have done this process, a sort of mantra, invoking the dream to come true. Bob Proctor and Peggy McColl had both told me to do this often and eventually it would come true as long as I held fast to the belief of it happening. When it did come true, my first reaction was, "You have to be kidding? This stuff really works."

Now that I have all the pieces in place to creating a multi-billion dollar entertainment franchise consisting of books, movies, theme park rides and merchandise, I realize how much control I have in manifesting my dreams. If I hadn't decided to go to the Bob Proctor event in Dallas back in the spring of 2014, I wonder where my life would have gone? Bob was right the first night of that seminar when he said, "If you apply these principles to your life and you dedicate yourself to the study of them, in a couple of years, you will need a telescope to look back at where you were before." Every day, I am grateful that I made the decision to go to his seminar;

it changed my life forever. There isn't a powerful enough telescope to look back at how I was living my life before. I have come so far and I love where I am going.

Is my life pre-determined? Is it based on circumstance or where I was born? Does my family or cultural heritage have anything to do with it? Absolutely not. The keys to mastering one's life is a raised awareness as to what active part you play in it. Each of us controls our destiny and we can live the life of our dreams. The way to do it is to decide exactly what you would really love to do then mustering the courage to do it.

ABOUT MICK

Mick Petersen is the International Best-selling author of *Stella And The Timekeepers*, soon to be a major motion picture produced by Oscar-winning producer Phillip Goldfine. His work has also been included in the International Best-selling book, Unwavering Strength. Currently, he writes, swims and enjoys island life in Galveston, Texas with his partner and fur-babies.

LIVING WITH INTENTION

BY ROBERT PASCUZZI

Destiny. I usually associate that word with a major historical figure such as Abraham Lincoln, Neil Armstrong, or Winston Churchill. It's easy to picture Churchill standing on a London rooftop with bombs showering down upon his city, defiant as a bulldog, almost as if he had been anticipating that moment his entire life. You may be wondering about your destiny, or feel you are at a turning point in your life. Perhaps you are confused or discouraged about your prospects. The truth is there are key decisions and fundamental changes you can make to direct the events in your life.

When I first began to look back on how I got from here to there, I thought it would be a simple exercise. I soon discovered that the answers were far more elusive than I initially presumed, but I was determined to dig deep so I could provide you with the most useful and honest information. As you will discover, I owe quite a debt of gratitude to the teachers who came into my life, and I am delighted to have the opportunity to share my knowledge.

I began by asking myself a blunt question: how did a kid who grew up in the little town of Urbandale, Iowa, who had never demonstrated any entrepreneurial leanings while growing up, and was a decidedly disinterested student who worked for years as an auto claims adjuster, wind up as a partner of Creative Planning, a company Forbes, CNBC News, Barron's magazine and others have named as one of the top independent wealth management firms in America?

There were also the "What if?" questions I asked myself. What if I had never met my wife, Kelly? What if I had never pursued a course in personal learning and self-development and instead settled for the status quo? What if I had listened to the coach who told me I would never amount to anything? What if I had decided to stick with the safety of a big insurance company, rather than take the leap to a firm that was blazing new territory, but had only been in business for a few years?

Twelve years ago, when I decided to join Creative Planning, many of my friends and colleagues wondered why I would abandon all the knowledge, relationships, status, and relative security of a large corporation and leap head-first into the unknown. After all, that's not something a guy with a wife, three kids, a mortgage, and a few car payments should do – at least not one who's in his right mind!

The truth is when I did make the move, I felt certain I was doing the right thing and it would ultimately lead me to tremendous success, although the next few years would be some of the most challenging years in my career as we built the business.

Due to my years of searching, questioning, learning, and training my mind to embrace the concept that the world is abundant, and with faith and gratitude all things are possible... I confidently made the decision. I knew if I was clear about my goals and focused on them relentlessly, it would only be a matter of time until I achieved them. I was also confident in my decision because I knew I was partnering with someone who operated at a high level of expectation and integrity. I believe our closest associations will inevitably come to define us.

I'll briefly tell you my story, and in the process, share a few of the principles I learned which helped me transform my life. This isn't only a story of business success but also one of gratitude and faith. Our lives are touched by many moments of grace, but we have to be willing to recognize fortuitous events when they appear, even though we may not appreciate them in the moment.

I was blessed with loving and hard working parents who instilled in me the importance of responsibility, honesty, and integrity as important attributes, for a successful life. My brothers and I didn't know any other way. Wealth comes in many forms and though we may not have been wealthy in financial terms, we were wealthy in our strong family structure. This was truly priceless and not something everyone receives. My parents made many sacrifices along the way, ensuring their children received a well-rounded faith-based education. They didn't spoil us and taught us the value of discipline and hard work at a young age.

After graduating college in 1986, I took a job as a claims adjuster with a nationally known insurance company. Did I take this position because I was passionate about it? Absolutely not! It was a job, I needed an income, and $17,500 per year sounded like I had hit the lottery! This attitude was a good indicator of my mindset and the low expectations I had for my life at that time.

My role with the insurance company was to visit the accident scene, investigate it, obtain the police reports, take the depositions of both parties, and try to settle on behalf of the company. I did this for approximately five years. Initially, I worked in Des Moines. After I was promoted to a supervisory role, I relocated to Kansas City.

The good news is, not too long after, I met Kelly, the love of my life for the past 22 years. Our mutual incomes allowed us to buy a small house. The bad news is I quickly realized how much I hated sitting behind a desk. I didn't like feeling caged in and I had zero tolerance for the politics with working for a big corporation. I stuck it out for a few more years because, like most of us, I bought into the conventional wisdom that said, "You may not like the job, but suck it up dude, you have the security of a regular paycheck." My decision to stick it out a little longer nagged me because I knew I was allowing a hole to be burned in my soul. That's what happens when you know something is wrong, but do your best to rationalize it.

A few years into my discontent as a supervisor, I began searching for answers. I read every self-help book I could find. Unfortunately, my school years left me believing I was not quite as smart as the next guy. But, guess what? I realized this mistaken impression I had of myself was only an old tape containing misleading information, programmed in my mind and running in my head for years. It was all false!

I'm a voracious reader and an avid student, but I have two conditions that traditional education rarely met: I have to be interested in the subject and the teacher has to have an engaging style. If these conditions aren't met

I quickly lose interest. We all learn in different ways, so we are responsible for learning in a manner that gets us excited about the possibilities in front of us. Remember, you owe it to yourself to constantly seek knowledge. Just like you feed your body, we must feed our minds every day.

I have always been something of a physical fitness freak. I enjoy starting my day by going to the gym. It was during this time I learned about training my mind while conditioning my body. I reasoned if I had achieved such solid results from a consistent workout program, then I could apply the same principle to my mind. I would head off to the gym every morning at 5:30 a.m. Armed with my Sony Walkman cassette player, I devoured teaching after teaching from some of the greatest personal development experts such as Brian Tracy, Wayne Dyer, Bob Proctor, Charlie "Tremendous" Jones, Jim Rohn, Stephen Covey, John Maxwell, Andy Andrews, Jack Canfield, Darren Hardy, and a host of others, including my greatest influence, Tony Robbins. What followed next was a significant shift in my attitude that eventually helped transform my life. It was during this time when I began to embrace the concept of what I call "Total Focus Conditioning."

• • •

Total Focus Conditioning. Condition your physical body and your mental capacities by starting each day with physical exercise while conditioning the mind. This can either be done simultaneously, or immediately before or after your workout. Mental conditioning consists of at least five minutes of focusing on what you are grateful for; then assess your short, mid and long-term goals, followed by affirmations related to your goals. For example, you may say: "I am all powerful, I am courageous, I am abundant in every good way, and I am a giver." Visualize your affirmations and feel the certainty in your body by making your goals real in your mind. By starting my day this way, my belief is I have already outworked my competition. When I say "competition" I am not just referring to other people, I also mean my greatest competitor, ME, or more specifically, my subconscious mind.

• • •

It was pretty soon after starting this discipline that it became obvious I could no longer ignore the uncomfortable burning truth in my gut. I knew I had to quit my job as a claims adjuster supervisor and find a sales position. You may wonder "What's the big deal?" The answer is, without sales experience, I had to start at the bottom selling insurance. I would not receive a salary. It was 100 percent commission, which meant some months I would make a decent amount of money, but other months, as the old saying goes: "Too much month at the end of the money."

Reluctantly, Kelly agreed it was time for a change. We held a bit of comfort due to the $40,000 nest egg we squirreled away for a rainy day along with the steady income from her job. It didn't take long for us to be thrown a curveball in the form of the birth of our first son, Alec, which meant Kelly had to quit her job. Alec was a tremendous blessing and another example of the abundance we are given in life. Regardless, it was a little scary at the time. Things rarely happened on our timetable, but we later realized God's timing isn't always our timing.

I became the sole supporter of the family, and my income was, at best, irregular. Our nest egg began to dwindle. It was around this time that I attended a Tony Robbins event in Chicago, called *Unleash the Power Within*. This marked a dramatic turning point in my life. Even though I had read Tony's books and listened to his CDs, the transformative impact of his live event accelerated my personal growth dramatically.

I learned an enormous amount that weekend. The last day of the event was the most impactful; Tony lead the attendees in a process that literally had the entire room moaning and crying. It was amazing to see thousands of grown men and women collectively confronting their innermost fears. Tony accomplished this by walking us through an exercise called "Dickens Process." He named it Dickens Process because it's based on a concept in the novel *A Christmas Carol*, by Charles Dickens. *A Christmas Carol* is about a man, Ebenezer Scrooge, who is forced to travel with the Ghost of Christmas Future. During their journey, Ebenezer Scrooge is shown two versions of his future: what will happen if he refuses to change and what could be, if he decides to change.

During Dickens Process, Tony had us identify our two greatest self-limiting beliefs. For me, it was the belief I wasn't smart enough, and a fear I would never have enough money, otherwise known as a "fear of lack." He asked us to close our eyes and imagine our lives over the next 5, 10, 15 and 20 years if we stayed committed to these limiting beliefs. We imagined how it would impact our families, our health, our relationships, and ultimately our destiny.

I felt physically ill. Against all my protective instincts, I began wailing with the rest of the crowd as I felt the accumulative weight of my current negative beliefs compounded over the next several years. It felt so real and powerful that it brought me to my knees. Imagine being at the most heart-wrenching funeral you've ever attended. Now, imagine it's your funeral.

Tony then walked us through the same scenario, where we shed our self-limiting beliefs and replaced them with new, powerful beliefs. When I left that night, I knew this experience had created a massive shift in my beliefs, and I felt my entire future would be altered as a result.

When I got home, Kelly could tell there was a change in me. I was energized by my new lease on life. My newfound energy allowed me to see all the opportunities before us. I couldn't wait to get started! I planned to "live with intention" and execute my strategies.

I remember telling Kelly I would meet Tony personally one day. So far, I had only ever given him a high-five at an event. It was only a matter of time before I met him; somehow, I knew he would play a role in my life. My beautiful wife simply smiled and shook her head, never imagining my prediction would come true.

I would like to tell you my career drastically changed right at that moment, but that wasn't the case. I had the lingo down. I could say all the incantations and affirmations, and practice my other positive rituals, but I didn't own it emotionally. Things began to erode and little-by-little, some of my old beliefs and fears about money crept back in as the bills piled up.

My new job as an insurance sales representative meant I spent a lot of time on the road meeting new people and selling – all the things that excite sales folks. The challenge was I was restricted in the products I was permitted to sell. In other words, I sold products that were in the best interest of the company, and not necessarily the best interest of the client. The other problem was the company retained a large percentage of the commissions, making it difficult to get ahead and stay ahead. Despite these concerns, I was most unhappy with how I felt about what I was doing.

I remember going out on a summer afternoon to meet with the owner of a fast food franchise. He was a wonderful, street-smart, and hardworking fellow who emigrated from Mexico when he was a kid. Due to his years of hard work, he was living the American dream. I persuaded him to purchase a whole life insurance plan as a means of investing for his retirement. The plan wasn't completely wrong for him, but if I was permitted to sell him other products, I would have found a more suitable plan. I didn't believe in the product I was selling, and I felt in my gut I wasn't operating at the highest level of integrity.

When you are determined to do the right thing for the client, even though it may cost you money, you are in sync with the Law of Abundance. If you approach your life with this mentality, you will ultimately achieve greater success; happy clients are your ambassadors and they will grow your business.

The gut-check didn't pass the test on days like that. Despite the fact I was continuing my daily discipline of personal learning, and had even attended a few more personal development seminars, I was sinking lower and lower. One particularly low point was when we had to put our mortgage payment on a credit card because we had spent our nest egg. We didn't have another option because all of our accounts were overdrawn. It was around that time I finally reached a breaking point.

Enough is enough!

Every night, I would go down to my home office in the basement to review my bank account online. I would review the checks that cleared, or in many occasions, bounced. I would total up the late fees, and stare at the screen, feeling paralyzed in horror. Looking back, it's obvious this routine was reinforcing my fears and magnifying the problems to the point where the solutions became invisible to me. It's almost as if I was hypnotizing myself with negative input. Can you relate to this? Do you dwell on problems and become so overwhelmed you can't find a solution? Does paralysis and negative self-talk set in? If so, then it's time to change the pattern.

I had reached a low point, but that's when something inside me burst free. If you happened to be looking through my basement window that night, you would have seen a grown man throwing a fit, tossing things around, and yelling nasty profanities. I finally shouted: "That's it. Enough is enough. I've had it! It's got to change and it's got to change now. I'm going to change this. It is within my control."

That must have been my lowest point because shortly afterward I started making fundamental changes to my behavior. I decided not to focus on what I didn't want to have happen. I stopped thinking and speaking about what I was fearful of and I only allowed myself to speak positive words and have positive thoughts. I would project things I wanted to see or experience. I imagined it before it happened. For instance, I would visualize myself with money in my bank account and visualize myself being able to pay my bills. I would visualize myself in possession of the things I desired.

Despite the positive changes to my life, I knew I had to fix my negative routines. For example, I used to hide bills. I would put them somewhere in my desk where I couldn't see them, but gave them more power. They became like a boogeyman lurking in the dark! I started laying the bills out on my desk where I could see them. I would place them in an envelope with a check. I would say to myself: "I'm ready to pay these bills. The bills are a good thing. There they are, nice and neat in their cute little envelopes with their little windows, all ready to mail with a check. The money is coming. I have all the money I need. I'm not worried about it anymore."

I'll admit it sounds a little nutty, but is it more sensible to constantly worry about something you can't change at that moment? Of course not! Worry is another form of fear, and fear will paralyze you. Fear keeps you stuck in your situation.

• • •

Create your personal visual goal book. I'm a visual guy, so I decided to create a goal book with pictures of things I desired to have one day. I described each item to a "T." I documented the type of house I wanted, including its colour and square footage. I included a red car with black interior. My visual goal book also contained pictures of my family and how their lives would improve. I visualized a lakefront condo and a cruise with my family. Through my goal book, I imagined the quality of education I could provide for my three boys. Over time I started to believe with 100 percent certainty the things I focused on could, and, more importantly, *would* materialize. My goal book became a big and powerful visual positive affirmation I could look at whenever I needed a boost, which was every day. Being able to touch my goal book made my goals seem more real.

Let me be clear about something: I love affirmations, but you would be delusional to expect results by repeating affirmations without taking action. You can't just sit in your bedroom all day and say "I'm rich, I'm rich,

I'm rich." You need a calculated and specific action plan that will lead you to your goals. In other words, you have to develop goods or services that can be exchanged for the thing you desire – money.

I still have my original goal book. It is so old it's held together with tape and rubber bands. It's a reminder of how my struggles forced me to search for solutions, so I can appreciate the dreams that have come true in my life.

• • •

My financial circumstances didn't change overnight. It was incremental. Every day things would get a little bit better. As I focused on the positive, my wealth increased and my life improved. Eventually, my ship set a new course. Let's face it, a bill is evidence we have abundance, which means we have something for which to be grateful. We have water. We have electricity. We have a home. We have a car. We have food. When you change your perspective, it is easier to evaluate your situation for what it is, instead of projecting fear and worry over something that will likely never happen.

Don't misunderstand me. I don't advocate minimizing serious problems or ignoring issues on which you should take action. I am saying needless worry creates fear, and when you make decisions in a fearful state, it often makes the problem worse. Define what is real and what isn't real, and take the appropriate action.

I'm talking about courage; something I think is in increasingly short supply in our society. Do you know people who are trapped in a bad marriage, unhappy in their workplace, refuse to abandon destructive personal habits, and consequently stay stuck in a rut of their own making? Are you one of those folks? If so, you should willingly embrace the things that frighten you and find a way to befriend them. Today is the day to define what you want and what you aren't willing to accept anymore. Then find the leverage to change. For me, it was the thought of not being able to provide for my family financially. You must find leverage for yourself, whatever it might be.

At last I have found my passion.

Some folks are lucky enough to know what they want to do with their lives from the time they are kids – that was not the case with me. I toiled in the workforce for almost 15 years before I discovered something into which I could put my heart.

I told you earlier I used to work for a big insurance firm which kept 60 percent of my earnings and instructed me to sell financial products that were only in their best interest. While I was working for them, I discovered the joy of selling 401K plans to small firms. The concept is now well-known, but I jumped into this field when companies were transitioning from fully sponsored pension plans and into 401K plans. I loved explaining the concept of 401K plans to groups of people. I enjoyed talking about the importance of saving for retirement, tax advantages, and principles of money. This made me a good candidate for this business. I believed in it because I knew I had found something that would be of tremendous value to my clients.

For those of you who may not know, a 401K plan allows the employee to save for their retirement while deferring the taxes on the amount they contribute. It also allows the employer to contribute to the plan. It is a tax-free way to increase one's income. It's a classic win-win for the employee because it is a painless way of saving, and if a company matches the contributions, it's a benefit that helps to retain valued employees. There are a host of other attributes about the topic that I am happy to share with you at another time, but suffice to say, when I found the world of 401K plans, I knew I had found my passion.

It was time to leave the firm. I needed to place my clients in investment vehicles that were in their best interest, rather than promote products that my employer wanted me to sell. I required the mental muscle I had built over the years to achieve the next step in my life. Although this was a major leap into the unknown, I was certain I was doing the right thing.

Do you remember earlier when I talked about moments of grace? The next event I attended was one of those times when fate stepped in to take my journey in a new direction, and it arrived in the form of my friend, mentor, and partner, Peter Mallouk.

Peter, the President and Chief Investment Officer of Creative Planning, is one of the smartest and most generous people I have ever met. He embodies an attitude of abundance, which I think accounts for his extra-ordinary abilities and his decisiveness. When Peter makes a decision to do something, he does it immediately. He doesn't wait until the next day. On one of our first sales calls, I learned that he also operates at a high level of integrity.

I joined Peter in the early days, when he only had four or five employees. I needed a desk and a phone to jumpstart my 401K business. During this time, I spent 95% of my day cold-calling, so, Peter agreed to rent me a cubicle.

The first few years were a constant struggle because the first question a perspective client would ask is: "How much money do you manage?" It was a complete joke. "Bob's 401K business" didn't take off until Peter and I figured out that we could leverage his connections and accounts. I got to spend a lot of "windshield time" with Peter and our friendship grew. I also had the opportunity to observe his work habits and fearlessness.

One day, I managed to cold-call our way into a meeting with a company that had a $100 million retirement plan. At that time, Creative Planning had only managed $100 million collectively. We were concerned they might ask about the size of our business. Regardless, we decided to give it our best shot.

I was sweating bullets when we got into the packed boardroom and, of course, it wasn't long before someone asked the obvious question about how much money we managed. I looked over at Peter, and he said: "Well, about the same amount you have in your retirement plan." Needless to say, we were ushered out the door.

My point is Peter didn't try to fudge the answer. Our only option was to tell the truth. The first few years felt like we were watching grass grow. We were making progress, but it was almost impossible to see.

• • •

Perseverance. It's times like that when you have to dig deep within yourself to be certain you are working harder and smarter. It's also when you need to toughen up and develop a commitment to perseverance. For example, most people think they know their physical limit, but the human spirit is much greater than you can possibly imagine. I proved this to myself around the time I was turning 40. I competed in the Iron Man Triathlon. The triathlon is a one day event that starts with a 2.4 mile swim, followed by a 112 mile bicycle race. It is capped off with a 26 mile run!

I managed to compete and complete it twice. The Iron Man Triathlon requires more than physical endurance; to be successful, it is more important to develop mental toughness, which I believe is within all of us.

I succeeded because I refused to quit, but many people who were in excellent physical condition gave up before they reached the finish line.

This was a transformative moment for me. I proved to myself if I set my mind to it, anything was within reach. I knew if I could finish the Iron Man Triathlon, I could master other aspects of my life, including my finances. You do not have to compete in a triathlon to prove to yourself that you can accomplish great things, but I'll bet there is something you have been putting off because your mind dissuades you. Don't let that happen.

• • •

There were days when I felt discouraged, but I believed in our mission. I believed in putting the client first. Regardless of your business, I advise you to embrace this approach. At Creative Planning, it's not enough that we charge the lowest fees, we also place our clients' interests *above* our own. By hiring like-minded employees who are experts in their respective roles, we help our clients make informed decisions. We operate with 100 percent transparency.

After several years, we had built significant momentum. Eventually, Creative Planning was ranked number 19 on the Barron's top 100 list. It wasn't long before other publications and financial media outlets began to take notice and we made other "best of" lists. This motivated us and we climbed up Barron's ranking to number 4. We now have the honor of being named Barron's #1 Independent Financial Advisor in America for the last 3 years! Today we are managing over $25 billion overall. In my division alone, we manage over $1.5 billion in retirement plans.

Believe it or not, that is when Tony Robbins came back into my story. I said before I always had the presentiment I would get to know him one day. That day arrived because Tony is on our board of directors as Chief of Investor Psychology!

The story of how Tony Robbins came to Creative Planning demonstrates exactly how the Law of Abundance operates. Tony discovered that he, and his employees, were paying excessive fees for their 401K plan. Unbeknownst to either Peter or me, Tony decided to look for the best financial planner in the industry which lead him to our company. Though it might seem like he was "at the right place at the right time," it didn't happen by accident. It was the result of years of effort, determination and perseverance. It was intentional!

I believe our lives are filled with moments of grace. They frequently pass almost unnoticed in the moment, but some are electric and obvious the instant they happen. The day I walked into Peter's office to meet Tony falls into the latter category. Tony is a presence, and a genuine force of nature. I knew something in my life had clicked into place the instant I grasped his hand. I sheepishly showed Tony my well-worn goal book, and, in his usual generous manner, he was blown away by it. We chatted for a bit, and eventually started discussing business. When the room grew quiet, I took the opportunity to say what was on my heart.

"I just want you to know that… You have been one of the most influential individuals in my life and even though we never met until today, you've had a significant impact on me." Then I looked over at Peter and said: "There are two people besides my dad who have impacted me the most, and I'm sitting in the room with both of them right now. This is a very special moment for me."

My hope is this story will encourage you to relentlessly pursue your dreams, see the blessings in your challenges, and always remember to live with intention. Live your **destiny**.

About Robert

In 10 years Robert went from no money in the bank – behind on his mortgage to building a 401(k) management division from zero to over $1.5 billion in assets, award winning author, speaker and coach.

PASSION

By Christine Lee

Des·ti·ny
ˈdestinē/
noun

1. The events that will necessarily happen to a
particular person or thing in the future.

2. The hidden power believed to control what
will happen in the future; fate.

When asked about his own destiny, Paulo Coelho, author of *The Alchemist*, said: "I can control my destiny, but not my fate. Destiny means there are opportunities to turn right or left, but fate is a one-way street. I believe we all have the choice as to whether we fulfill our destiny, but our fate is sealed." While this book is one of destinies, it often feels as if my destiny happened to be fate all along. Over the course of my own journey, I made many decisions along the way that led me to my fate, but in hindsight, it always seemed like I was headed in one direction, and one direction alone. In the end, it often feels like my destiny was my fate.

I wasn't born in America. But a series of decisions, maybe even destiny, brought me to this beautiful country. I was originally born in South Korea, and came to the United States with my family just after turning 14. My father had already immigrated to the US, but we remained in South Korea. However, because of substantial political turmoil and unsettlement in my home Country, we decided to leave. So, we followed behind with my mother and siblings and came to America. We arrived from a small village in South Korea, and culture shock would have been a nice way to describe our experience. The US offered me and my family great opportunity, but it was quite a transition for us all.

There were substantial changes occurring back home, and we were all feeling the burn post-World War II. We experienced great poverty, but my father's job offered us the occasion for change. He was a translator for the US army, and worked to assist American soldiers to understand Korean during the beginning of the Vietnam War. That offered us the chance to advance in life, and receive a strong education in the US.

We were a Christian family, and my mother always considered herself to be a daughter of God. She was extraordinarily humble, and worked hard to raise each of us with strong character and high morals. Surrounded by poverty in South Korea, that wasn't always an easy task. I still remember my mother tending to the homeless within our neighborhood, offering them food and water. She would care for them, and would never turn them away. She'd greet them, and make every single one feel like he or she was the most important person in the world. It was her gift, and her generosity trickled down to her children. My mother was often sick, but that didn't stop her from always putting the needs of others before her own. She had terrible Asthma, and was regularly on an oxygen tank, gasping for her breath as if it would be her last.

Even then, I still remember awaking each morning to see my mother praying. She would start her day extremely early, 4:00AM or so, and begin her daily prayers. Mom did this until she passed away, and it instilled a sense of purpose and faith within us. Faith quickly became an important part of our belief system. We weren't always old enough to truly understand to whom we prayed, but we easily recognized just how crucial maintaining a strong belief system was to our parents. So we followed in tow, and respected the wishes of our mother. As the siblings grew, faith became an important part of our existence and relationship with the world around us. Perhaps it was blind faith that led me in the direction of my destiny.

As I entered my adult years, I carried a number of different jobs. But I was a real estate agent on the day I met my destiny. I can still remember almost every detail, able to paint a vivid picture of it every time I close my eyes. It is ingrained in my mind, and I will never forget that fateful car ride. A close friend of mine owned a rickety car, and it was always breaking down. So it was no surprise he called me on a warm California day, asking that I give him a ride to see a friend of his. I agreed to pick him up, and he asked that I take him to a small school outside of California.

He told me of this school on numerous occasions. He also indicated he thought I should consider meeting the head-master. My friend went on and on about the school, offering me detail after detail, indicating he thought it would be a great place for me to work. I had never once thought of entering the educational realm, so I thought his request to be completely silly. But as we drove the thirty or so miles, he started in again. We jokingly exchanged jabs at one another, as most friends do, eventually entering into the driveway of the school. I intended on pulling in, having my friend jump out, and then moving on to the listing appointments I had scheduled for the day.

As we pulled in, my friend insisted I come out of the car and survey the quant little University. Begrudgingly, I agreed to do so. As I exited the vehicle, my friend grabbed my hand and said, "This is the University you will be working at." I laughed at the statement, and then followed him up the driveway. As I approached the entrance of the school, I saw a large red and white sign, with the name of the University emblazed on the front in a deep red color. I saw a small mission statement etched under the name. It said: "At the University, out students not only learn to find success, they learn how to give it meaning – in the classroom, studying abroad or through volunteer work. It's all about getting the most from your college experience – so you can get the most of life." For whatever reason, I smiled upon reading this statement. The University seemed like a nice place, but surely not one I intended on staying at for long.

As we made our way to the entrance of the University, the head-master greeted us. She was a middle-aged women that seemed to be exuding energy. The head-master immediately introduced me to her. Before I could even say "hello," my friend said: "Hi, this is Christine. She is going to work at your school." I couldn't believe my ears. At first I thought this was some kind of joke. But the women's response was not indicative of any type of joke. She appeared to be completely serious and focused. As I looked around, I realized my friend had retreated into the school. I was completely isolated, alone with this woman I had just met. And she meant business. She said, "Christine – thank you so much for coming. I know this may seem crazy to you, but I would like to give you the keys to this school. I need help, and our mutual friend has told me he thinks you can run my school. I was confused. I said, "Thank you so much. But I do not want to work at a school, and I certainly do not want to run one. I have no experience in education, or running much of anything. In fact, I am not even looking for a job. This is all very strange. It is so kind of you to offer me this opportunity, but this is not for me."

She responded. "I have run this school for 35 years. This is not for me anymore. I am tired and aging. This calls for excitement and energy. You have both of those. Please, we have money in our operating account to run the programs. We have dozens of students enrolled, so more tuition money will be coming in."

In that moment, the head-master reached into her pocket and pulled out a single key. She took my wrist, and opened my hand, placing the single silver key into my palm while still grasping my wrist. We both looked down together, and then our eyes met. I felt drawn to her. For some reason, I wasn't able to pull away, even though I was much younger than she. She then closed my hand, and I clinched it into a fist, with the key in the middle. She asked me to come back on January 12th, just a few days later, to take over my position as the head of the school. It all seemed like a complete world wind, and I stood there dumbfounded and speechless.

But education meant so much to my family and me, and I knew my mother would be proud. So, I decided to do it. I agreed to take over the school, and return just a few days later to begin running the show. In that moment, I went back and forth between sheer fear and excitement. It seemed like a wonderful opportunity, but who starts their day as a real estate agent and ends it as the head master of a University? My real estate business was slow, so it wasn't a great loss. I figured I'd jump right in and do it for a year or so, and see what happens.

But as you know, sometimes you have to be careful what you wish for. As I began my work at the school, I came to realize there were many problems with the University. The staff was pleasant and the students enjoyed the learning process. However, we'd receive regular correspondence from the State Government that regulated the school. The agency exists to promote and protect the interests of students and consumers: (i) through the effective and efficient oversight of California's private postsecondary educational institutions, (ii) through the promotion of competition that rewards educational quality and employment outcomes, (iii) through proactively combating unlicensed activity, and (iv) by resolving student complaints in a manner that benefits both the complaining student and future students.

You'd think the governing body would act as our ally, but I came to understand there was a substantial amount of tension between the faculty, Dr. Kingston, and the State. Even then, I did everything needed to ensure the University followed the rules and regulations outlined by the Government. I registered the University, and ensured I had all the necessary pieces in place. There was a great mess to clean up, and the letters continued to pour in. I came to find out that the Government was challenging our accreditation, which presented a substantial problem for us. Without our accreditation, we could no longer operate as a University. We would have to completely shut down. While I had just started my job there, I decided I would fight to keep this University open. I couldn't quit explain it, but I just felt connected to the University and all the wonderful opportunities we offered the students that attended.

As I approached the mailbox each and every day, I relished at the thought of the continued correspondence from the Government. With each passing letter, it appeared we were edging inches closer to having no choice but to shut down. It almost felt as if there was a target on our back, and the Government was firing warning shot after warning shot at us, getting closer and closer to hitting the bull's-eye. I opened the mailbox and my heart sunk as I saw yet another letter with the Government notary on the envelope. I riffled through the rest of the mail and quickly tore open the letter. It was my worst nightmare. The letter indicated that the University would have no choice but to close down on March 15th, 2013. A Government attorney wrote the letter, and it indicated they'd sue me and file an emergency injunction if I chose not to cooperate with their demands.

I couldn't believe it. I was falling in love with the school. I enjoyed awaking and driving to the University, greeting the students and closely working with the faculty to implement new curriculum. And now they wanted to take that away from me. I hadn't wanted this in the first place, but now that I had it, I couldn't let them take it away. I wasn't a lawyer, so I didn't understand why they would close the school on me. Their problems were with the previous owner, Dr. Kingston, and I had nothing to do with those issues. But unfortunately, the State decided to take out their anger out on me. I learned that Dr. Kingston carried quite the reputation with the Government, and he faced 31 different violations during his time as owner/headmaster. And I would have to pay for his mistakes.

I thought of my options, and decided I would not close the school. They'd have to come put the lock on the door themselves. It took me numerous lawyers and tens of thousands of dollars before I found an attorney willing to fight for me. We began reviewing the case together, and through our correspondence with the Government, learned that they believed the Dr. Kingston was a fraud. They thought the University was selling degrees, and only issued less than ten legitimate degrees since its existence. The accusations were substantial. The case seemed to be daunting, so much so that my lawyer recommended I just settle with the State, and move onto something else.

But I couldn't do it. I just couldn't quit. This was my destiny. I had made the choice to take the school, and I had to deliver on my promise. So we decided to fight, and not give into the threats of the Government. I continuously argued with my lawyer about the case. He thought I was an idiot for fighting. He didn't see a path to victory, only defeat. But he agreed to fight, even though I knew he only did it for the money. Even then, I knew I did nothing wrong and ran an honest and morally sound program. From day one, I instilled the character in the University that my parents taught to me. We would not give in for the sins of our fathers.

The trial was set to begin in October of 2015. I was nervous, but I always felt a sense of calmness through the process. On the first day of the trial, I told my lawyer I was scared. He told me I could still throw in the towel. There were times when I wanted to just quit. It was scary to face the unknown and the enormous resources of the Government. I knew I was outmanned and couldn't keep up. But deep down in my heart, I felt a strong purpose. I owed it to my students, my faculty, and my family. I would do all I could. I would fight. The show must go one.

For purposes of scheduling, the case was eventually reset to March of 2016. The trial then began, and the Government called several witnesses against the University. They detailed the allegations to the judge, and outlined the specific violations, one after the other. I was scared and in complete shock. I couldn't believe how real it all was. But I remembered the words of my mother: "God will watch on you from the front, not from the back." These words kept me strong, and I continued. The trial lasted for weeks, and during one of the shorter breaks, I enjoyed coffee with Bob Proctor, my mentor.

I met Bob at a coffee shop in Los Angeles. I sat there, sipping coffee, while Bob enjoyed a sandwich. He inquired about the trial. I was hysterical. Through tears, I told him:

"I think it will close down. No one is helping me. My lawyer's more scared than I am. What do I do?"

He didn't respond. He continued to eat.

"Bob – I'm all alone. No one is listening to me. I have nothing but my school. I gave up my career for this. I have nowhere to go. Next Monday will probably be my last day. They will close me down. Are you even listening to me? Bob? Bob?"

He still didn't say a word.

"Bob, are you listening to me? Are you really listening to me, Bob? Do you know that my school's closing down? Is there anything that you can do for me? Can you tell me? What can you tell me?"

Finally, Bob finished his sandwich and looked up at me. He smiled and said: "Christine – write down what you want."

That's it. After all that, that was all he said. I responded: "What do you mean write down what I want? I can't just write this down. What are you talking about?"

He looked at me again and said: "Just write it down."

"All I want is for the school to remain open. I want the Government to leave me alone and let me run my school. That is it."

Bob said: "Then write it down. Don't forget to also write down what you are happy and grateful for. And don't forget 'thank you' at the end. Once you write it down, your turning your whole universe around within the world. And write it down 3000 times."

I almost laughed. The trial was set to begin again in just three days. How could I write this down 3000 times in just three days? But I decided I would at least try. I looked at Bob and smiled, still thinking this wouldn't really work. But I left that coffee shop and went directly to the University. I walked into my office and I wrote down the following:

"I am so happy that the school remains open. I am so happy that the litigation is over and I am the new owner. I am so happy I can provide these wonderful children with an education." And then I wrote it again and again.

Over the next three days, I spent almost every waking minute writing down that statement. I thought my hand would fall off. But I did it. And on the last repetition, I took the small piece of paper, folded it up, and placed it in the pocket of the jacket I would wear the next day in court.

I was hopeful Bob was right....

My trial started again the following day. More witnesses. More testimony. More of the same. I was still scared, but I put my hand in my jacket pocket and rubbed that small folded piece of paper. As the day ended, my lawyer confronted me and said: "Christine, I'm just letting you know that if we don't show up tomorrow, you'll be okay. You'll be out of everything. You don't even have to be here. We can pay the fines, and you can close the school. One day, you can open a new one. It will be ok."

But I refused to listen to him. This was my choice, this was my destiny. I told my lawyer I would show up. I asked that he sit beside me and have faith. God will let me win. He called me an idiot. As we appeared in court the next day, we took our places and awaited the Judge. The Judge took the bench, and asked that both my lawyer and the lawyers from the Government approach the bench. I could tell by his facial expressions that he was upset. What more could I handle? He then motioned for the lawyers to return back to their respective desks. He then looked up and said the following:

"This case has no merit. The Government has no case here. You are suing the wrong person. She did not commit these violations. Dr. Kingston did. Where is he? Why didn't you bring him to court? Why would you waste the court's time with this nonsense? This case is over. I am dismissing the allegations and closing this matter. The University can continue to operate so long as Ms. Lee is the new owner and has no ties to previous management."

And then like that... it was done. Bob was right. I was right. My faith was right. My choices were right. My destiny was delivered. But I wasn't alone. Another destiny was sealed that day.

Just a few months after my trial concluded, I went to the mailbox that rested in front of the University. I used to dread this moment each day, awaiting yet another letter from the Government. But that was no more, as the University continued to operate and enrolling new students. I opened the mailbox, and immediately saw a letter from the Administrative Board. The letter indicated that the State was shutting down the governing body that sued me. I couldn't believe it. The same governing body that tried to shut me down was now shutting down itself. As I said, two destinies were sealed on that day in court. As of the publishing of this book, the University is enjoying close to full capacity and regularly graduating students with post-secondary degrees. It has become an environment for learning and cultural development. I am proud I didn't give up. I am grateful I did not succumb to the fear I felt. It wasn't always easy, but mentors and support appeared when I needed it the most. While I know much of what occurred did so because of my choices, I cannot help but think my mother and her faith guided me along the way. Perhaps I was destined for this, but it always seemed like an unexplained force was guiding the path. It might have been destiny, it could have been faith. But I am grateful for whatever it was that drove me to close my hand around that key. That moment now allows me to work diligently as an educator to shape the destinies of our students each and every day.

About Christine

Christine Lee is an extremely creative being who has dedicated her life to being of service, has influenced countless lives with her thoughtful writings, empathic strength, and developed courage. As a businesswoman for over thirty years, she has an established reputation for integrity, valor, and honesty. She is energetic in the studies of personal growth, emotional, spiritual, and psychological development, and passionate about empowering others to realize their beautiful destiny. She's committed to turn her dreams to reality, setting up paradigm shifts in the educational foundation, and adding value to next generations to serve.

MANIFEST YOUR SUPERHUMAN CAPACITIES AND GREATNESS

By Dr. Jussi Eerikainen

"Everything is energy and that's all there is to it."
– Albert Einstein

To say I grew up as a science and math geek would be an understatement. It must be true if a film about electron microscopes caught my eye as a young boy, and held my attention during class. The moment the vibratory rate of electrons, neutrons and protons explained matter, life suddenly made sense to me. At that moment, Albert Einstein became my idol, and I swore I would grow up to become a nuclear physicist just like him.

Being small for my age, skinny as a twig with saucer-sized spectacles and a genius level of understanding in math and science certainly contributed to my perpetual ridicule. After the film finished, none of the other students shared my enthusiasm, so their bullying of me continued. The fact that my classmates didn't accept my idiosincrasie was unimportant to me; I was focused on bigger issues. I wanted to understand how the world worked. Specifically, I wanted to understand how a boy with a tragic and tumultuous past fit into the whole scheme of life.

In 1936, long before I was born, the Soviet Union invaded my family's homeland in Eastern Finland, forcing all inhabitants to flee or die. My parents were part of the wave of refugees that poured into Helsinki. They lived poorly in the cramped and filthy living conditions of a crime-ridden city, a stark contrast to the peaceful forests filled with plentiful fish and game to which they had become accustomed. My mother gave birth to her three children, my two sisters and me, while my father scraped by, bouncing from one menial job to another. They fantasized about the good life back home, and hated the Russians who displaced them. These less than ideal conditions forced them to make a difficult decision – separate their fledgling family for a time so that my father could seek out a suitable home abroad. He boarded a ship, and set out on a globetrotting mission in pursuit of a better life.

In the jungles of Colombia, South America, a British gold mining company hired my father, promising him a good salary and safe housing. The rest of us waited for months until he had finally earned enough money to send ocean liner tickets to make the long journey to join him. The hot and sticky air slapped our faces as we disembarked in Cartagena. The inhabitants, strangely dressed people, ate bizarre food and spoke a language none of us could understand. If Albert Einstein said everything is energy, I wondered, 'What frequency was I on to arrive here?'

In the 1940's, leftist guerrillas funded by my father's nemesis, the Soviet Union, moved into the jungles of western Colombia, disrupting the mining operations. Fidel Castro arrived to organize their efforts to attack the foreign companies working there, which destabilized the whole region. When a higher paying job was offered in Bogotá, my father snatched it and moved us to the capital of Colombia, ensuring our safety and security.

We adapted quickly to the urban environment. We loved exploring the new parks, museums and markets. I particularly liked the new private school I attended. Unfortunately, after some time, the violence from the mountains moved into our adopted city and riots stoked the insurgents that broke out in the local streets. Bogotá became so unstable we were no longer safe. The Americans approached my father, and enlisted his help in their efforts to defeat Jorge Eliecer Gaitán, the leader of the Communists, and the destabilizing forces he led.

Before my father agreed to assist the Americans, he sent my sisters away while my mother and I packed suitcases for our escape. The Communists had once again forced my parents to flee, and my parents hated them for it. On April 9, 1948, Gaitán was killed. He was originally scheduled to meet with Castro on the afternoon of the day he was murdered. The city erupted in violence, an event which is known today as Bogatazo.

As retribution for my father's suspected involvement in their leader's death, an angry band of commando guerrillas kidnapped the three of us. They blindfolded us and drove us deep into the mountains. When the vehicle finally stopped, we were pushed from it and forced to stand in the rain. Our hoods were removed and the commander gave the order. "Kill them!" he shouted. I watched in horror as my parents were forced to their knees and executed right in front of me, something no ten year old child should ever have to see. A man behind me held me back as I crumpled to my knees. I was in shock. My world took on a surreal quality. Tears and rain fell in droplets, and mixed with my parents' blood, which had pooled in the mud around me.

For some unknown reason, my life was spared, but all I wanted to do was die. I was dragged to my feet and forced to march in the pouring rain for hours. Eventually, we reached a makeshift camp where I was put in a cage like an animal. For the next 10 days, I was numb, reliving the atrocity of my parents' death over and over in my mind. I cried until the tears stopped coming. A cook, a middle-aged woman with long dark hair and a sympathetic look in her eyes, took pity on me. One evening while delivering my meal, she whispered, "I can help you escape if you promise to follow my directions exactly as I tell you." Considering that my life had been filled with violence and bloodshed over the past few days, I looked at her with suspicion. "Trust in me," she said, "I will help you."

As it turns out, one of the guerrillas was in love with her, and she used his desire to convince him to cooperate with her as she schemed to help me escape. It was a way for him to earn her affection. He gave her the camp schedule. Having knowledge of the comings and goings of the other guerrillas allowed her to plan my escape perfectly.

For the next few days, nothing happened, and I began to doubt her intentions to help me. One evening at dusk, she brought my dinner for me as usual. She set the plate of food on the ground and looked me square in the eye. She said, "It's time to make your escape." With my hand in hers, she led me away and gave me instructions.

"Tell me again," I pleaded. She shook her head no, and shushed me.

"But I don't understand."

"Don't worry," she said, stopping at the edge of camp, "you'll understand my instructions when you need to."

For a few moments, I stood looking at her, wondering where an angel like her could have come from. Out of the corner of my eye, I saw a man move toward us. I froze.

"Run!" she yelled as she pushed me into the dense forest.

Suddenly gunfire erupted all around me, ricocheting off tree trunks on either side of me. I ran as fast as I could, knowing that my life depended on it. Somehow, I avoided being hit by the bullets that whizzed past my ears. On my right, I saw the steep embankment she had warned me about in her instructions. I tumbled down it and found myself in a jungle so thick that I could see nothing but shadows. I quickly located the wooden trunk tucked away in the underbrush, just like the cook had told me, and I hid in it.

Loud shouts and heavy footsteps of the banditos echoed off the trees. Tremors of fear coursed through me as I held my breath. Every time I heard a sound, even the slightest sound, I thought my hiding place had been discovered. As time passed, I pictured the horrible possibilities of what could happen to me, and I wondered if I would survive this ordeal. I squeezed my body deeper into the dark corners of the hidden trunk and prayed I would make it out alive. Convinced that my destiny couldn't end this way, I pleaded with God to let me live.

Of all things, a frog finally gave me the courage to attempt an escape. This little guardian angel calmly climbed onto my arm and wouldn't leave. His peacefulness bewildered me. I discovered that my fear was inside of me, not outside. The frog didn't feel fear, so it must be something I was creating internally. His calm energy gave me three ideas that I've held onto ever since: everything is energy; no matter the situation, as long as I maintain a calmness of mind, I'll get through it; everything is in my head, and I have the power to control situations with my thoughts.

The moment that I decided to release my fear, a feeling of confidence that I would survive this ordeal came over me. It was as if I finally felt safe. I knew that my escape was imminent and guaranteed.

Long after nightfall on a rainy night, the lid of the trunk creaked as I pressed it open. After two long days stuffed in the box, standing up hurt my bones. My little green friend jumped onto a nearby branch and stared back at me, his iridescent eyes aglow. "Go in peace," he seemed to say.

Scurrying in the shadows, like a fox through the unfamiliar landscape of the mountainous jungle, I made my way to a small village. Despite feeling weak and dehydrated, I mustered enough courage to knock on the door of a house. The woman who opened the door understood my plight immediately without any explanation on my part. The nuisance of the guerrillas had wreaked havoc on the villagers. She gave me food and something to drink. She hid me away until she could arrange a bus ride for me with her brother back to the capital.

The long bus ride was made longer by the possibility of encountering the guerrillas again. With every bump in the road or pump of the brakes, I feared being recaptured and taken back to their camp, or worse, killed. When my thoughts wandered to this dark place, I redirected them to the frog, and the fear passed.

At the main bus station in downtown Bogotá, the driver made everyone disembark. He informed me that he would take me back to the only safe place I knew – my school. It was located in the far northern suburbs of the city. It was not on a bus line, and it was a long way from the bus station, but he chauffeured me there anyway. With profound gratitude, I shook his hand as I stepped onto the sidewalk. A cloud of black exhaust churned from the exhaust pipe as the bus disappeared down the road.

The next morning, the headmistress found me curled up at the front door of my school. She cried tears of compassion as I recounted my story. She, and the other staff members felt sorry for me, and introduced me to a wonderful German family who took me in and raised me as their own.

From then on, I felt cared for and safe. Normalcy returned to my life in the form of a daily routine. The personal tragedy of losing my parents beset me, but I forced its retreat to the interspaces of my mind. Only at night when I felt the most alone in the world did I dare to reflect on it. For years, I cried myself to sleep. Questions popped into my mind about why such an injustice had happened to parents and me. Had my unusual upbringing somehow prepared me to face the trauma of my parents' murder? Did my family's displacement and relocation to a foreign land equip me to deal with the chaos I had experienced? Could living without my parents somehow make me stronger?

Around this time, I came into possession of a recording by Earl Nightingale called *The Strangest Secret*. Its message mesmerized me the first time I listened to it. Thereafter, I would run home after school to listen to it over and over, believing every word that Mr. Nightingale recited. By listening to this recording as often as I did, my life began to change. I buried myself in my studies, and my grades slowly improved. The bullying stopped, I made friends and, for the first time ever, I gained confidence in myself. A blanket of calmness also descended upon me, much like it had when I encountered the frog in the trunk. Even though my family was gone, my loneliness disappeared. Mr. Einstein's statements about how energy is everything gave me a glimpse into the reasons. In the deepest part of my core, I felt connected to something bigger. An awareness of an ever-present invisible energy emerged, and I wanted to understand it.

Instead of pursuing my ethereal interest in energy at college, I chose to study mathematics. Deep down, I accepted that my secret passion of nuclear physics wouldn't pay the bills, whereas teaching math would give me financial stability. I also knew mathematics was a prerequisite to become a nuclear physicist just like my idol, Albert Einstein, so I endeavored to become good at it.

Poor health had plagued me all through my education. At the time, I saw no correlation between bad eating habits and bad health or bad thoughts and sickness. It never occurred to me that my poor health could be untreated post-traumatic stress disorder (PTSD) manifesting itself in my physical body. To better understand my health, I felt compelled to study medicine in graduate school. I wanted answers, and I wanted to cure myself. It was a career choice where my strength in math and science would be used to its highest potential. I eventually earned my Doctor of Medicine (MD) with a specialty in Cardiology.

After completing my residency, I saw patients in a hospital setting, until I opened my own practice. Throughout my clinical work, an interesting phenomenon revealed itself; I observed very sick people heal themselves. The medical community called them 'anomalies' because no scientific reason existed to explain how their conditions improved. This occurred at a time when my knowledge of the power of the mind was still in its infancy. I investigated these miracles to prove there existed a mental science whose power surpassed all the pills and potions available. Soon I was prescribing the deliberate use of mental exercises combined with energy frequencies and brain waves to heal people. In fact, I even began using them on myself.

I observed the behaviors and results of my patients and myself, and I wondered what was creating such miraculous outcomes. "Could it be related to the invisible energy that had caused so many changes in my own life?" I pondered. I hypothesized that it must influence every aspect of our lives. It expressed itself in every reaction, every response, and every interaction that I observed. It caused, or at least affected, everything. I recognized it in the behaviors displayed toward relatives, dramas played out between friends, lovers, and co-workers, and through acts of kindness and aggressions that are so evident in society. It even helped me cope with my parents' deaths.

I started playing around with the idea that human beings were frequency emitters, like individual beacons, broadcasting signals like radio towers. But, how did it work? More importantly, how could these frequencies be used to change or improve the results of the common man to help them have better lives?

Questions like these led me to discover what I refer to as the signature frequency. Deep within each one of us is a blueprint of energy. Like the genes of our physical body, this code of energetic DNA makes up our signature frequency, transmitting an energy signal that attracts to us every event, situation and experience in our life. As these signals (our behaviors) go out, responses (our results) come back. Without effort and guidance, the default settings would be in control. This explained why my patients had experienced miraculous healing of their conditions. I wondered if this energy could be passed on to our children in the same way physical traits were passed down. In other words, was this invisible energy hereditary?

I got my answer while reading a study. At Emory University, researchers discovered how animals pass along traumatic and stressful experiences to subsequent generations through morphic fields. Morphic fields are the energy fields which give us our shape and certain behaviors. During their tests, they exposed laboratory mice to stressful and alarming stimuli while releasing a cherry blossom scent into their cages. The mice became conditioned to equate fear with the aroma of cherry blossom. As it turns out, this conditioned response was passed down six generations. This experiment proved that behavioral patterns of these rodents were shaped by the conditioning of previous generations. Hidden triggers concealed within the morphic fields of the mice dictated the behavior of their offspring for six generations!

Relating this research to the human experience, I began to see how the tragedies in my personal life affected my results in life, as well as those in my patients' lives. I began to ask, "What if the events and choices of parents, grandparents or even further back in the family lineage could affect us?" I quickly realized the answer was yes! Suddenly, I understood, and I was able to explain why people behave, respond, and react the way in which they do.

Many behaviors have nothing to do with us because we didn't consciously chose them! Instead they have everything to do with the conditions and circumstances of our forefathers. Much like our physical DNA, we have an energetic DNA blueprint that expresses itself uniquely in every person. No two frequencies are alike. Every person has their own individual signature frequency. This is why we find fractures that lead to self-sabotaging or self-defeating behaviors which hold us back from achieving goals or living the lives we yearn to live.

There's good news! With proper action, it is possible to discover and eliminate the undesirable behaviors that don't serve us, and repair the fractures. Fragmented, broken, separated, tormented and torn frequencies held within our signature frequency can be changed. Everyone has the power to become a wholly, self-realized human being. But, can these repairs in energy translate into physical changes?

As few as 20 years ago, scientists still believed that the number of neurons, and their configuration of networks in the brain, were formed during the first few years of life. It was believed that once they were set, it was permanent, which meant we would not have the ability to grow new ones.

When neurophysiologists and neuroscientists examined the brain in a more detailed manner, a better picture of what was happening came into focus. The neurophysiologists and neuroscientists used more sophisticated technologies to track brainwave activity with X-rays, MRIs and other equipment. Researchers noticed that the brain would change its physical structure with repetitive thoughts and mental exercises. This explained why my life changed when I listened to the Earl Nightingale record over and over! My brain had become supercharged.

Today, scientists are finding higher capacities in human beings – and this means ANY human being – that start to develop by simply pursuing a path of introspection, self-growth and development. These new capacities are radically different than anything ever seen previously in human history. For the first time, human beings are beginning to lose the fear factor. This is not only a new development today, but a first-ever-recorded phenomenon never before seen over the course of human history. All of a sudden, it's as if the lid on possibilities has been blown off. All sorts of images of a better future started to generate themselves.

One of the most common thoughts regarding these new developments defining humanity can best be described as extraordinary. By integrating all these components into our being, we, as a species, are simply moving beyond the traditional characteristics of our past human capacities in a profound way. Our psyches are coming together as a whole, and in a genuinely holistic way into a life of wholeness, a life of meaning, a life of purpose and a life of value.

Knowing what we know now, there's finally an explanation for the positive results I have achieved in my own life. Although I accidentally changed through repetition, I cannot help but think that an invisible force had somehow guided my transformation. Mysteriously, I was lead to make changes in my life through repetitively thinking new and different thoughts. My mental faculties became stronger and more dynamic through use and exercise. I had unexpectedly tapped into a source of knowledge and an intelligence deep inside myself that I didn't know existed.

Scientists have now identified at least 15 different human intelligences, all of which display various perspectives and dimensions, and once activated, can improve who and what we are as individuals. Our entire beings can undergo an evolutionary shift from that of being partial, fragmented, broken and torn, to one of being unified, integrated, whole, harmonious, peaceful and powerful. This explains why we are losing our fear factors, doesn't it? This is such a radical change to our common human evolution. Through use and mental strength building, these intelligent capacities have been shown to manifest themselves at extremely high levels. It looks as though an evolutionary lightbulb is illuminating in each one of us right now. We only have to flip on the switch.

When changes occur to the brain's structure, there are a whole host of other changes that occur in regards to potential, intelligences and dimensions of being. We are not just working with IQ and cognitive intelligences anymore. Instead, we find that we are working with a whole spectrum of different types of capacities, intelligences and emotional moods, which each one of us possess.

When you combine all these elements, you realize that the brain can be trained to adopt these potentialities as their standard default settings. When you take these different powers, and you understand that they all go through stages of ever increasing betterment, excellence and capability, and know that if you work them up into their higher ranges, you get an adaptive and malleable brain with a default setting locked into these higher ranges. This is when one goes from having a normal human capacity to what, without any exaggeration at all, is "superhuman."

Since retiring from my medical practice, I have started studying energy full-time. I have come full circle in my life – from the childhood trauma of losing my parents to my true passion, the study of energy. Currently, I devote all my time to studying how the proper understanding and use of this vital energy can change mankind, and how it can benefit all of us. My best-selling book, *Transforming Vibes, Transforming Lives* (available at amazon.com) details many of my findings and discoveries.

Our brains are capable of adapting. They can be restructured and reconditioned to produce superhuman results in whatever endeavor we decide to undertake. Each one of us has the ability to use all of our intelligences, and to achieve great things far beyond that which we could have ever imagined. When we realize this, suddenly our superhuman powers spring to life, our true greatness manifests itself into reality and we are able to realize our destiny.

Our world – technology, science, medicine – is changing rapidly! I believe it is possible to transform our world even more, giving us all a brighter and more hopeful future, especially if we understand that we are all interconnected to each other and connected with everything in the universe. More importantly, human consciousness is changing faster than anything else. The only question that remains unanswered is, "Are you willing to accept the challenge to change yourself and your responsibility in this change?"

During my years in my medical practice, I prescribed energy to heal my patients. By healing others, I have healed myself. With my own experience of trauma and the resulting PTSD, I've discovered methods to deal with and improve PTSD by improved lifestyle choices, better ways of thinking and a proper mindset. Today, I educate healthy people about how to achieve their highest potential using this energy. By helping humanity to find a better way of life, we have an opportunity to change the world.

ABOUT DR. JUSSI

Losing his parents from Finland at the age of ten in a tragic way, Jussi Eerikäinen was eventually adopted by a loving, nurturing German family. After studying Mathematics at Los Andes University in Bogota, Colombia he strongly realized that he had a different calling into the medical field. He then went to study Public Health at the Loma Linda University in California. Then, for more than thirty years, he practiced both traditional and alternative methods of healing in Venezuela. The Universidad Nacional Experimental de Guayana (UNEG), in Puerto Ordaz, Venezuela, asked him to create special programs for physicians and psychologists, based on his methods of treating patients with energy, frequency, and prevention. Now, he has decided to share his wonderful methods with the world by writing books. He is living in his dear Tenerife, Canary Islands, Spain, where he is still creating, writing, and designing programs to change humanity's destiny.

IN THIS MOMENT

By Rachel Bazzy

I consider all children as precious gifts, and of course, my children are the most talented and beautiful gifts in the world; and don't even get me started on my adorable grandchildren! Then there is our dog, and the magnificent trees on our property, even the tiny Hummingbirds that we feed. I consciously choose to love life, nature, laughter, people… continue the sentence in your own mind. Think about what you love! I look for the beauty in all things, something to be grateful for in every instance, and above all, I value that indomitable spirit that lies within all of us.

As each of our three children were born, I was in awe of their perfection, and the very miracle of their birth. In an era before 3D imaging sonograms, and in their own time, they each materialized on the outside what I had felt growing on the inside. The What became a Who. What parent hasn't admired their handy work, cooing over physical genetics, perceived talents, anticipated personality traits, attributes, and future achievements? When our first son Eric was born he immediately lit up the delivery room. Red and screaming, weighing in at almost eleven pounds, he was impressive, even for a newborn. The delivery room exploded with energy. I had given birth to a supernova. He was destined with magnificence, a knowing that I would hold in my mind and encourage him with, his entire life.

Eric was passed from nurse to nurse, each person wanting to hold him in turn, weighing him with their arms and their hearts. Finally, a nurse brought him over to me, prefacing my viewing with a forewarning remark that startled me.

"Now, he's got a little something on his arm…" her voice trailing off in concern, as she tugged his right arm out of the receiving blanket. He was still screaming. My heart pounded, hearing the tone of her voice and his loud, vociferous protests, my attention was suddenly focused on his health. She carried him over to me and there, on his little, chubby forearm, was a brown, triangle-shaped mole. At that moment, with a huge sigh of relief, I placed a kiss on his birthmark and reframed her remark.

"Ah, no, that's where the angels kissed him!" I prayed to God for a son, and here was the gift. I attracted this stellar child into our lives, and I loved him with all my heart. I still do.

I did *not* attract the death of my son. I did not, nor could not, control the actions of the stranger who caused his death. This was not God's will, fault or desire; God did not look the other way, punish me or cease to protect my child, so that I could have a better understanding of the Law of Attraction.

What I *do* attract, is who I am, now. I attract that on which I focus, and in what manner I choose to view things. How I process this fatality and all the other moments in my life, through my own thoughts, emotions, imagery and desires, attracts more of what makes me who I am today. So, I choose to be strong. I choose to have courage. I choose my destiny.

Humans have free will. We all have the ability to choose our thoughts, to examine our beliefs, and analyze our mind. There is a wealth of information at our fingertips, a path of learning, a wonderful journey of growth, if we have the desire to learn. We do not have to settle for mediocrity. We need not be habitual. We do not have to suffer.

Most of us have read or heard stories of other people in crisis, or we may know someone who has suffered a loss. Today's news is filled with trauma, catastrophe, tragedy, and misfortune. Perhaps you, at this moment, are suffering with something in your life, frustrated, struggling, living with fear and doubt, uncertainty and despair; settling for less than who you are made to be.

I am sharing my story with you, to offer you hope. There is a light at the end of the tunnel, and it is within *you*. It is that spark in your Spirit which, upon encountering calamity, rises up from the fragments of life, using the strength of will, and turns the desire to survive, into a life of thrive. You can choose the destiny of your outcome. I am. And now I am going to share with you a glimpse into the dark tunnel I have come through.

"NO! NO! NO! NO! NO!" I screamed, as I pounded violently on the lid of the toilet where I kneeled in anticipation of vomiting up my denial and anger. In the hallway, my husband collapsed down the wall into a heartrending crumple, sobbing uncontrollably. The phone call that no one ever wants, the call that no parent should ever receive, came from an unknown number in a familiar, local town. A call, which I knew instinctively, was about our son, and so I answered. A chaplain from the little town's hospital, was calling to delicately inform us that our thirty-two-year-old son, Eric, was dead. I knew how, before the man tactfully explained that it was a motorcycle accident, for our family shared the love of riding. Traumatized, I handed the phone to my husband Chris, and stumbled to the bathroom.

"I JUST GOT HIM BACK!" I exclaimed, now visibly shaking, as my body processed what my mind could not. I salivated as my heart pounded in disbelief. I was angry. I felt cheated. I refused to accept it. Our beautiful son, who was finally back in our lives after years of alcohol and drug abuse, was gone? *NO! NO! NO!*

In that moment, as I spat into the toilet, the emergence of irony surged through my mind. All those times when we thought he could have died from an overdose or the multiple suicide attempts, all the incidents of crime, violence, arrests, restitutions, rehabs, anger, disappearances, and second chances; the eighteen years of hell on earth he put himself and our family through, and now that he is sober, happily married and has it all, he is gone? Unbelievable. Unacceptable.

Numbness. Incredible sadness.

Close family and friends immediately aided with their support and love. My phone blew up with hundreds of messages. Innumerable condolences flooded my social media, untold prayers whispered for our family, heartfelt cards, mementos, and flowers were received. Then, there were the fringe; those past acquaintances and strangers who trickled in their inappropriate texts, allegations, private messages, photos, clichés and gifts; those which incited my anger, and polluted my emotions. But in this fire of chaos, the lessons from our studies kicked in. Anger and pain could not burn away our education, our wisdom, nor our ability to choose.

You see, my husband Chris and I have been on a learning journey. Several years ago we chose to invest in ourselves through education; we are constantly reading and studying. We have attended many self-empowering events, listened and studied materials by Tony Robbins, Bob Proctor, Napoleon Hill, James Allen, and Raymond Holliwell, to name a few. We are gaining knowledge, and implementing skill sets and tools. Each of us is discovering our higher Self, our destiny, along the way. We have walked on fire many times. Striding across hot coals is a symbolic tool for teaching the power of the mind, facing fears, and seeing new possibilities. If I can do that, what else can I choose to do?

It was during a Tony Robbins *Date With Destiny* event, that I set my top goals, of which one was to express myself as a professional author. But my greatest, emotionally fused must, was to get our son back. I visualized his healing. I knew the magnificence he was born with, the energetic, intelligent child whom we had raised. I could see him attending events like these, and exploding out of his old paradigm like a supernova. I knew his magnetic spirit, his charismatic strengths, his leadership capabilities; I knew his potential and saw his future. I saw our future. Eric would finally be the man of his true destiny; our family would be reunited. Once again, we would enjoy the nucleus of love, laughter, happy chaos, and the dynamic of our family restored. I would write the story, our story. I felt pure love, and I could feel Eric, once again, in that special place in my heart. Like all of my children, he was a part of me. I knew his heart; he knew my heartbeat from within.

In that moment, I chose to forgive the past; all of it. I chose to stop focusing on the pain, and the negative impact of Eric's drug induced behaviors, and just let it go. I exchanged suffering over Eric for reclaimed, unconditional love for him. In an instant, I changed my paradigm, my vibration, and my destiny. My heart felt light, my spirit soared. I continually practiced what I had learned. I forgave myself. I forgave him. I loved myself and I focused my love and energy towards him. I visualized his smiling face, his silly nature, his bear-hugs. I missed him, yearned for him. I got emotionally involved with the meditative words, when I whispered, "Eric, Mom loves you and I am never giving up on you." I believed. I knew I would get him back.

A few months later I 'accidentally' received a text Eric meant for his younger brother. I smiled. I *knew* it! My heart pounded. I was euphoric.

The past two years of distance, hatefulness, and absence were soon going to be over. I typed a response, identified myself, and asked if we could forget the past and start over, he and I. Holding my breath, my finger hovered over the send button. My heart was pounding. Hey, I walk on fire… I got this.

Eric and I spent the next six months rebuilding our relationship. At first, I told no one, not even Chris. I had such joy inside; it was my little secret, like being pregnant and not sharing the news for a while. I savored every moment, every text, the sound of his voice. We sent each other photos. We shared plans for our new bikes, riding together and our love of music. We traded silly memes and laughed at stories. He told me all about his precious wife, his family, his great job, and his sobriety journey. I shared with him photos of his childhood, his Dad and I, pictures of our new home, and shared with him our journey. I told him I had a ticket for him to a Tony Robbins event, and he was looking forward to attending. I told him I was proud of him, and that I was seeing the man I always knew he could be. I was seeing my dreams becoming a reality.

Chris and I began studying with Bob Proctor and Sandy Gallagher, through books, videos and on-line seminars. Coincidently, we were participating in Proctor Gallagher Institute's live-feed seminar, *Think and Grow Rich*, the same weekend we were reunited with our son. Eric and our daughter-in-law stopped in for a visit, on their way home from a weekend ride with their Serenity motorcycle riding club. I made dinner and we all sat together as a family for the first time in two and a half years, laughing and sharing, making plans for our future, and once again hearing "I love you" from our son. Chris and I were witnessing our positive thoughts, mental pictures of restoration, and actions of unconditional love manifest before our eyes. We got our son back, through our own attitudes, forgiveness, and courage to trust. The Law of Attraction works.

Both Chris and I gratefully relish those moments spent together with Eric and Gillian; grateful for the reminiscing, our laughter, adoring their relationship, sharing his embarrassing baby pictures with her, and taking family selfies. Those were our last photos together. Within three weeks, he was gone.

Five months later, Chris and I were in Toronto, attending Proctor Gallagher's Matrixx seminar, refocusing on our goals, and the methodology for obtaining those goals. We have infinite gratitude for Bob Proctor, Sandy Gallagher, and their team of wise professionals and consultants, who have all been instrumental in our evolvement. One of the first assignments I was given was, for 30 days, handwrite the last chapter from *As a Man Thinketh*, by James Allen. The chapter is titled, *Serenity*. I still write it out, every day.

It is no coincidence that during this event, exactly five months from the date of Eric's death, I met Peggy McColl. Peggy is a *New York Time's* Best Selling Author and an internationally recognized speaker, author and mentor; she is an expert in the area of goal achievement. As Peggy spoke to our Matrixx class, I felt such a connection with her, and such a desire to work with her. I didn't know how it would transpire, but in that moment I *knew* that my destiny as a writer would be coming to fruition. As Peggy introduced the concept of the *Destinies* project, I recognized that Eric's story *would* be published, and the writing and publishing experience would propel my destiny as a professional author. I am very grateful when I say that today, with Peggy McColl as my mentor, my objective is to help others, using my wisdom, imagination and infinite energy from our Creator.

I wrote our son's obituary, and read it aloud at his funeral. Arrangements were made, photos and music chosen; hundreds of guests greeted and consoled. I stood alongside our daughter and younger son, held hands with my husband, and touched Eric's birthmark, kissing my baby boy for the last time. Later, next to our daughter-in-law, I endured the sound of brass casings hitting the concrete, the 21-gun salute echoing through my soul. In this moment, Eric was being honored for his service to our country. He was no hero, but he was courageous. He didn't see any action, but he fought many battles. His resilience was a testimony to his inner strength, his death as tragic as it should have been.

We choose to live in gratitude. It's that simple. As the saying goes, "Pain is inevitable, suffering is a choice." We choose to be grateful for our son's life, for all the lessons we have learned from being his parents, and for the growth and contributions we make because of those lessons. We choose to focus on the good in his life, to focus on the What, not the Why; focus on What we do with our lives from here on. We choose to move forward, with the understanding that it doesn't mean we have forgotten our son, but that we each have destinies yet to fulfill. Eric will always be a part of our destiny.

I encourage you to examine your own thoughts, beliefs, and emotions; think about your relationships. Consider your dreams, and your current destiny path. Let go of the negative, the bitterness, perceived injustices, the blame, guilt, fear and pain that holds you back. Find something, *anything* and everything for which to be grateful. Contemplate the miracles, discover the gifts, and raise your awareness. When you change your thinking for the better, you change your life. Read, study and grow. It is all waiting for you to explore and the journey is awesome.

In this moment, in my spirit, I hear Eric saying, "It's O.K., Mom, use it all, write it all." Eric never gave up. It takes courage to pick yourself up, time after time, to rise from darkness and explode into a new life. Eric's tenacity and courage have been incredible gifts to me. Because I found the courage to dream and make changes within myself, I have attracted the means with which to share our message, which is, never, ever give up. In this moment, make a decision. Develop gratefulness. Strive to cultivate your intelligence. Think. Open your mind, learn and grow. Direct your energy towards your dreams and goals, and to those you love, including yourself. And live. Live the beautiful **destiny** that you can choose to create.

About Rachel

Rachel Bazzy is an extremely creative being who has dedicated her life to being of service, has influenced countless lives with her thoughtful writings, empathic strength, and developed courage. As a business woman for over thirty years, she has an established reputation for integrity, valor, and honesty. She is energetic in the studies of personal growth, emotional, spiritual, and psychological development, and passionate about empowering others to realize their beautiful destiny.

To learn more, visit www.rachelbazzy.com

YACHTS OF FUN

By Wendy & Keefe Ditta

The clock was ticking, and my heart seemed to be beating faster and faster as my senior year of high school was coming to an end. I was full of anxiety as the days kept getting closer and closer to graduation day. While others knew what colleges they were going to attend and what careers they wanted to pursue, I on the other hand was clueless and with this realization panic set in. I honestly had no idea what I wanted to do with the rest of my life. I didn't give my career much thought, thinking that I would just go out and get a job after I graduated. I wasn't a model student with excellent grades, in fact, I had never even read a newspaper or a book in my life, plus four years of college never really did appeal to me.

One day a teacher went to each class selecting certain students and with me being one of them I found myself on a bus going down Engineers Road. Well, Engineers Road is a business district with a variety of opportunities in pipe fitting, welding, offshore, crane operator, etc. As I looked around the bus, paying close attention to who else was on the bus, I soon realized that the students selected were not considered college material. It was like a career field trip as we drove down the street while the teacher pointed to the left and then to the right at the various businesses for us to fill out job applications.

Well fortunately, for me, our air conditioning system broke at home. My dad called in an Air Conditioner (A/C) repairman and within 45 minutes and a cost of $350.00 later our unit was fixed. I thought for a moment and decided wow! That's what I want to do. I shared the news with my parents and later enrolled in a school nearby to learn the A/C and heating trade. I was truly engaged and interested in learning the trade and I had dreams of opening my own business. Two years later, I graduated and bought a $600.00 used truck from a telephone company auction. With a tool belt around my waist and a used truck in my possession, I placed an ad in the phonebook with what seemed like the last dollar I had… before I knew it, I was in business!

I had no formal business experience or business education, but what I did have was the absolute desire to own a successful air conditioning and heating company. It wasn't as easy as I thought it was going to be, after all, I knew air conditioning, not business. I thought overhead was anything over 7 feet. I had a lot to learn, and even with having to learn the hard way, I refused to give up on my dream. There was never a plan B, it had to work, it had to be successful. Well, one thing for sure, I was very successful in creating a job for myself. For the first twelve years, I considered myself self-employed, I did all of the work myself, and because my business was seasonal, I had a pocket full of money in the summer and I was broke in the winter. I kept falling into that same hole, doing the same things and receiving the same results. I didn't want to let go of what I knew how to do. I wasn't willing to stretch myself because I enjoyed meeting new customers, servicing and replacing new units, and I was really very good at it too.

Deep down inside I knew I wanted bigger and better things in life and in business too, but the business model I was following was not giving me the results I desired. After twelve years, I took myself out of the production role and began seeing my business from a whole different light. The only way I was going to grow my business was to hire people to do the work. There was no way I could grow it as a one man operation, and no matter how hot it was, there was only so many hours in a day that I could work. It was very hard for me at first because I prided myself on the type of work and service I provided. I didn't think anyone could do it as well as I did, but there was no way I was going to grow my business by trying to do it all. I moved my business from my garage to a huge warehouse district. I placed ads and hired service technicians, installers, warehousemen, a delivery guy and a few people to work in the office. My company finally felt like a real business. I had to learn how to run it like a real company too, and quickly, as the business was starting to take off.

When I met my wife, Wendy, she brought a sense of professionalism to the office. She's an organizer and Heavens 1st law is order. As it turns out, the stackable trays I was using weren't a very good filing system. She came in and put systems in place that helped the flow of business move smoothly. Together we developed ideas, strategies and new ways to pay people with incentive programs – work became fun! I didn't mind not being in the field any longer. I loved running my business. I loved the collaboration we had and the fact that we both shared the same vision. She has always been my biggest supporter, and always encouraging me to go for it, whatever it may be. Today we are one of the largest residential A/C & heating companies in our area. We have always been willing to share our business success, software and ideas with other A/C companies with the intent of them becoming more successful and never feeling like we were in competition with them.

Although everyone's road to success is different, I never saw myself as an entrepreneur, but I do enjoy opening businesses and creating a vision for them. In August 2005, hurricane Katrina struck our area and it sure seemed like every A/C unit in the city was under water. We were installing new units day and night. It turned out to be one of the most successful years we ever had, and that afforded us the opportunity two years later to invest in a few condos on the Gulf Coast. We didn't feel like our condos were being managed to their fullest potential, and decided to open up our own rental management company.

I said, "I don't know anything about condos, but I do know how to run a business."

We started off small by only renting out our 3 condos but the vision I had was to be the largest rental management company on the Mississippi Gulf Coast. Through dedication and persistence, within a few years, we achieved that goal. Today we are renting out over 250 condos, and we are the largest rental management company on the Mississippi Gulf Coast.

I've had my eye on a 51' Leopard Catamaran Motor Yacht for years. I found myself checking out the different floor plans and dreaming of us taking it to the Bahamas. It wasn't until May 2015 that I seriously considered ordering one. I started doing some research and contacted a broker in Fort Lauderdale who later sent over specifications and information. He called me one day to inform me the new owners of the exact type of yacht that we were interested in would be in town on a certain weekend to do a sea trial on their yacht, and that they didn't mind if Wendy and I joined them. We were excited, and of course we said yes, and couldn't wait to make all of the necessary plans.

It happened to be the same weekend we were flying in to Port Canaveral for a cruise. We couldn't get over how perfect the timing was and decided to fly in a few days early to enjoy some time in Florida. We stayed at a small hotel near the beach. The porter that helped us with our luggage asked us how many days will we be staying. We said only two.

He laughed and said "This is a lot of luggage just for a two day stay."

I filled him in on our great news about how the sea trial of the yacht fell right in place with the timing of us flying to Florida for the cruise. His reply was, "The universe must be on your side." My wife and I looked at each other with huge grins as we were both thinking the exact same thing: who says that? Not everyone talks about the universe the way we do.

The next day we met with the broker and the owners and we set sail on their new yacht. We were grateful to physically experience this opportunity. We visualized ourselves as if we were on our very own yacht enjoying the wind blowing through our hair, the warmth of the sun on our skin and the feeling of gratitude in our hearts. While sailing, the broker mentioned it would take ten months to order a brand new 51' Leopard Catamaran, and that he actually had one already in production, scheduled to be completed in just four short months. Our plan was to pay one-million dollars in cash, but at the ten-month mark, we felt like we were stretching ourselves. The idea that we could actually be setting sail on our very own yacht in just 4 months was beyond exciting and scary at the same time. We both sat there quietly contemplating what we just heard.

The broker said, "Go on your cruise and think about it. Call me when you get back, but I will need an answer by next Sunday."

We went to dinner and neither my wife nor I said a word about what the broker mentioned earlier. When we got back to the hotel, I asked her what she thought about the broker's offer about buying the yacht in production rather than buying the one ten months from now – she just gave me a look.

Then she asked me "Hey, what's the name of that chapter you've been reading for the last ten months?"

I laughed and said with a very deep voice, "Decisions" (from *Think and Grow Rich*).

She then said, "Well, I think you need to make one."

We went on the cruise and I couldn't stop thinking about how perfectly things had lined up for us in order to actually see and experience the yacht in person. I certainly couldn't just ignore what the porter said to us about how the universe must be on our side. All of this played over and over in my mind continuously for the next week while we were on the cruise. I kept thinking that if I just break it down to two smaller amounts I only needed $500,000.00 from each business, which was only $125,000.00 per business per month over the next four months. The next day after we returned home, I wired a 90K non-refundable deposit with the remaining balance due September 24, 2015.

From the moment I made the decision to buy the yacht and wired the money, I knew that my goal would begin to manifest. From that moment on, as I worked towards my goal, I made each day a successful day. The very first thing I did was write out a goal card that said: I am so happy and grateful now that I have earned enough money through multiple sources of income to pay for my new 51' Leopard Catamaran by September 24, 2015. I kept it in my pocket as a reminder of my goal every single day and I wanted to be aware of it at all times. As soon as I wired the money, I knew I was manifesting the end result of acquiring the funds needed to purchase the yacht. Every New Year's Eve, my wife and I would sit in our Jacuzzi, watch the fireworks and make a toast to our new dreams and goals for the upcoming year. For the last five years, we would always say that we needed to get smarter with our money. Well, setting this goal made us do just that. It made me a better businessman and together we eliminated all waste within our companies and at home, staying on top of the financials daily. Recognizing that every day can either be a success or a failure, we did everything we could to make each day a successful day. It's amazing what you can do once you really put your mind to it.

In 2015, both of our businesses had the best year and that wasn't by accident. Our persistence had paid off, and by September 24, 2015, we acquired the money needed to pay off the balance owed on the yacht.

Today my wife and I are living the life we have always dreamed of, and now we are dreaming even bigger. We always knew that we were **destined** to achieve success and together, we have not only created thriving businesses, but we have created the life we were destined to live together. Successful people often say if I can do it, you can do it too. We realize that to some people that may be hard to believe, but I am here to tell you that I started with a $600.00 truck, a burning desire and belief in myself.

To desire is to expect and to expect is to achieve.

About Keefe & Wendy

Keefe Ditta is the founder and president of Keefe's air conditioning, heating and electrical.

He was born in New Orleans, La. and graduated from Archbishop Shaw High School in 1977.

In 1979 he received a degree in the a/c & heating trade from Delgado Community College and opened his business later that same year. He and his wife Wendy are the owners of 3 successful businesses from Louisiana to the Mississippi Gulf coast.

Wendy Ditta was born in Metairie, La. and graduated from John Ehret High School in 1984.

Keefe and Wendy enjoy spending time with their family and especially enjoy playing with their 3 year old grandson, Colton. They enjoy traveling, reading, studying, serving others and spending time on the water in their new yacht, Persistence.

THE DECISION THAT CHANGED OUR WORLD

By Naveed & Sonika Asif

All newlyweds have a dream of how their life is going to be after marriage: a great big house, great income and a beautiful loving family. Our dream was no different. We (Naveed and Sonika) wanted to travel, earn millions through a big business we built from scratch, have a beautiful family with two kids and a little beagle running around.

Six months into our marriage, things weren't going as planned. We were stuck living with our parents, we had no income, and we were still trying to come up with the right business idea. We were constantly feeling low and confused, until one day we decided to sit down and have a serious talk about our future. If there was one positive thing we had in common, it was we weren't afraid to ask for help when we needed it. We decided to register for some personal development courses in order to better ourselves and figure out our passion.

We began our personal development journey with the Landmark Forum. Going through those three days seemed to give us some clarity and helped us dream a little bigger… but the second we went home, it was like someone pushed the reset button on our mind and we were back to our old selves again. We thought, "Okay maybe the Landmark Advanced course may give us what we're looking for." The Advanced course taught us to be more in tune with others, and for us to always be in the space of making others feel good, because that's how we feel good. Still, something was missing; we weren't feeling that burning desire within us.

Our next step was to attend a more business-oriented course, so we registered for the T. Harv Eker's *Millionaire Mind Intensive*. At this stage, we realized we needed to change our 'money blueprint': all our past beliefs, ideas and conditioning about money and success. But how exactly do we change it? We knew we needed to start a business and systemize it to earn a million dollars, but we still didn't know how to change the beliefs in our subconscious mind. We kept asking ourselves, "How do we change the habits that are holding us back?"

It was one year into our marriage and we couldn't believe the changes that had occurred: absolutely none! Zero! We were still living with our parents, had no income… we were both lost and confused. We gathered all kinds of great information, but we didn't do a single thing with it. It was extremely frustrating because both of us liked working 9-5 jobs, and we refused to give in to that vicious cycle.

One day as we were browsing the internet, an advertisement popped up that had to do with binary options trading. The ad stated that unlike Forex trading, we simply had to predict the direction a currency or stock was heading and we could earn up to 90% returns on our investment. Being desperate at this point to earn some sort of income, we researched more into it. We chose a broker, opened a demo account, and started trading. A few days later, we received a call from one of the company's agents who convinced us to invest $25,000. We decided we needed to take a risk if we wanted to change things, so we used the money received from wedding gifts towards it. We decided to invest another $25,000 because trading was working out great.

The time had come for us to step out and be on our own. For us to be focused and move forward we needed to live elsewhere. We asked our parents to help us out with $2,700 a month which would cover the rent of our new place, and other monthly expenses. We packed up our stuff and moved into our new home, ready and excited for our trading business to take off. Our wedding gifts was completely gone at this point, but we figured we'd make it back from trading, right? Wrong!

As soon as we deposited the $50,000, things seemed to go a little eerie: trades were always going in the opposite direction, and our agent always had some excuse for the trades not working out. Our $50,000 account was down to $18,000 and to make matters worse, we couldn't even withdraw this amount until we met their terms and conditions. Eventually, we were out $50,000, with nothing left in our bank accounts. A lot of fights, crying episodes, tantrums, worry and frustration followed. All of this was putting a strain on our relationship, and to make matters worse, our parents were going through some financial troubles and were finding it difficult to continue supporting us. It felt like we were stuck in a dark cave and losing sight of the light at the end. Although things got worse we never lost hope. Something within us knew we were destined for greatness and we weren't going to stop until we found it.

We decided to search for something that could help us improve at trading while earning our money back. We joined two Facebook trading support groups which shared with us a trading system that brought us better results. Unfortunately, it wasn't giving us the explosive results for which we hoped. Determined to improve our results we invested in every educational trading course available until we finally figured it out.

As we hit the one-and-a half-year mark in our marriage, we were still extremely stuck, and way off in terms of our beautiful life plan… but we had learned a lot of valuable lessons along the way. One day while waiting for our dinner to arrive, we decided to turn on *The Secret*. Although we had both seen it many years ago, we felt the need to watch it again. I guess we were hoping it would help us break out of this situation. The first man that came on the screen was Bob Proctor… and something about his energy really resonated with us. We started applying the principles from the movie in our lives by setting up vision boards and visualizing what we wanted to achieve. We printed a cheque, wrote *$1,000,000* on it and signed it with our names. We were excited for our life to finally change and take a turn for the better. Not too long after we started attracting small things into our life such as affiliate opportunities, parking spaces, better relationships with friends and family… but where was the big stuff? Where was the house, the big business and what about the million dollars? Once again, we were left scratching our heads, wondering what we were doing wrong.

We decided to look deeper into the teachings of Bob Proctor, the one person that truly resonated with us from *The Secret*. While watching his *Science of Getting Rich* seminar YouTube video, there was something he said that completely blew our minds. He said, "If you want to change your results, you have to stop looking outside of you and start looking deep inside your mind." That was a brand-new idea which really got us thinking about where we were in life. We had been so stuck on what our bank account said, that we didn't realize that our own minds, our own beliefs and our own habits were causing that bank account to remain the way it was.

Curious to know more, we headed to Bob's website to learn about his coaching program – instead we came across an opportunity to work with him as his certified consultant. This was a chance for us to help spread the wonderful information that he teaches. It was as if a bunch of bells went off in our heads after reading through his website, and we realized that this was the burning desire for which we had been looking: the chance to help people live a truly fulfilled life and for us to live in abundance in the process. We quickly filled out our information and waited for a call.

Two weeks passed and we still hadn't received a phone call. We were getting impatient so we decided to call them ourselves. We spoke with Chris, one of the sales people at the Proctor Gallagher Institute, who explained the process and the program we would be selling and coaching people through. It sounded perfect, but at the same time we knew working with a man like Bob Proctor meant we were going to have to pay a big price. The cost to become his consultant was a whopping $18,500. Now keep in mind we lost everything we had in that trading account, and we were being supported by our parents. We were both thinking the same thing, "How on earth are we going to pay this off? Where is the money going to come from?"

We asked Chris to give us a minute as we stared at each other. We both knew we wanted to do this and we knew it was the right fit for us. Suddenly, in that moment, something remarkable happened. We felt a burst of fear and anxiety rush through our body, and we began shaking – but we also felt excitement rush through us at the same time. There was an enormous conflict that went on inside of us and we knew we had hit the terror barrier big time. Without saying one word to each other, we knew we were going to do this. We didn't know how, but we didn't care. We just knew we would figure out a way. We got our credit card, made the payment, and hung up the phone… and that's when all hell broke loose. We started jumping up and down, wondering what on earth we had just done, and how we were going to find $18,500 when we weren't earning a single cent. We had put ourselves in such a situation, that it was either sink or swim from this point on.

We decided right then and there that we were going to swim, and we were going to push harder than ever before to make this work. We dove into Bob's material and started studying every second of every day. We let our burning desire drive us to such a point where we didn't care what people thought of us. We didn't care if people rejected it or if they didn't believe in us. We believed in us, and even more so, we were ready to leave behind the dark hole we had been in for over a year. We started visualizing the $18,500 in our bank account as we worked hard replacing all doubt, worry and fear in our mind with thoughts of prosperity.

We picked up the phone, set appointments with everyone in our phone book, and started teaching and selling this information. Even though some of our enrollment conversations were complete disasters, we didn't allow it to slow us down – we had a purpose. We had a vision of where we were going and we kept pushing. In the 30 days that followed, we registered 7 people into the program, which brought us to $21,000. Not only did we find a way to pay off the credit card payments, but we also made more than we needed.

As a year passed by, we started looking for ways to increase our standard of living. As we developed more of the success mindset, we knew our dreams weren't just going to fall into our lap. We had to do something about it, so we decided to begin with our dream home. We knew exactly which penthouse we wanted, we knew the million-dollar price, and we knew that our families would think we were crazy. That for us was enough proof that we were moving in the right direction.

We contacted the real estate agency and went to see the place. It was perfect. A two-story penthouse with windows that went all the way to the ceiling, tons of natural light, huge space, three bedrooms and two beautiful balconies. It was exactly what we wanted. We arranged for a meeting with the owner to see if we could negotiate a deal. The owner told us we needed to make a down payment of $110,000 and after that we could pay the remaining balance of $900,000 however we wished. Knowing we would have access to some money in six months, we agreed to the deal. We found a way to pay the down payment, signed the sales purchase agreement, and went to work looking for furniture.

Keep in mind, we had no clue how to pay the remaining $900,000. Our parents were beside themselves, thinking we had lost our minds…

because who in their right mind would sign a sales purchase agreement for $900,000 when they had no idea how to pay that amount? We didn't allow this to discourage us because we knew one thing – the laws are always working in our favour. It worked for us before, and it will work for us again. In the six months that passed, we didn't give even one second of thought that we won't receive the money, or it won't become available to us on time. We just kept living as if the home was already ours. Five months later we received a call from our lawyer who told us the money would be available to us earlier. It was in our account a week later and just like that, we paid the remaining $900,000 cash payment in full. One month later we moved into our dream home.

The most important lesson we learned from those moments was that we made a quick and serious decision to change our life. Napoleon Hill said that "Successful people make decisions very quickly and change them very slowly, if and when they change them at all." We had made decisions like successful people and didn't even know it; but we sure did reap the rewards.

Today we are one of Bob Proctor's top certified consultants worldwide. We are living in our dream home and we have two adorable little Beagles to welcome us home every day. We finally figured out that our destiny, life purpose and passion is to change the world. We are abiding by the laws and following the universe's plan every single day – and you can do the same. You're destined for greatness; it's in your nature to grow and expand your awareness every day because you are a part of the same universe.

It took one decision to change our life – a decision to finally follow our **destiny** and allow ourselves to become the amazing people we are. We know beyond a shadow of a doubt, if you start making decisions without worrying about the resources, you're going to see an amazing shift in your own life as well. Start doing what you're destined to do and be the change you want to see in the world.

ABOUT NAVEED & SONIKA

Naveed & Sonika are the first in Thailand to ever be certified by Bob Proctor & the Proctor Gallagher Institute, and the first in the world to expand globally. They quickly rose to become one of the top consultants in the world and have already changed hundreds of lives worldwide. Our mission is simple: If you can tell us what you want, we can show you how to get it.

NAVEED ASIF

Being born in Bangkok, Thailand, Naveed has inherited the culture of being compassionate towards people and helping them. While working in his family business, he joined a networking marketing company in the Wellness industry. He joined a self development course called The Landmark Forum. Today, Naveed is helping people locally and globally transform their lives like night and day.

SONIKA MADARASMI ASIF

Born and raised in Bangkok, Thailand, Sonika was always known as one of the smartest kids in school. She broke her first barrier by attending Academy of Art University in San Francisco to complete her Bachelor of Fine Arts in Fashion. She then went on to work at many fashion jobs: fashion stylist, model booker, fashion magazine column writer, and production assistant. After marrying her husband Naveed in 2014, Sonika began her journey in personal development. Today, Sonika is living the life of her dreams by helping people all around the world break out of that 9-5 rut and finally enjoy this beautiful journey called life.

ANGELS IN THE COURTROOM®
FROM A CIVIL LITIGATOR TO A SPIRITUAL TEACHER

BY ESPERANZA UNIVERSAL

Travel with me 20 years back into my destiny. I'm in a courtroom, litigating a case in the Superior Court of the state of California. The case is an exciting one. The courtroom is stale and cold, with dark clothing being worn all around me. Even the walls are plain and neutral in color. The attorneys and the jury seem so somber; it feels like a funeral, with a strong sense of control and authority. As a child in the courtroom, it was terrifying. It seemed empty, lonely, cold, and damp. It was huge, I felt small and lost. Wow, it's so different for me now, as an adult.

Several years prior, I would have been terrified of the very idea of being in a courtroom, as it was my home as a child. I was a ward of the court from infancy, shifting from foster home to foster home, institution to institution, and then off to another home, or should I say house, as none felt like a home. Not really knowing why… why was I different? Why didn't I have a family like everybody else, or a home where I could stay, with parents and siblings, those who cared? I didn't know, I would just hold my breath, and move from system to system without question, without conversation. My life was at their whim. They could do what they wanted. I was a piece of furniture that could be moved from place to place without concern to anyone. The courtroom held terrifying memories for me.

As a child, the courtroom was cold, dark, lifeless, and scary. I vowed to turn off, feel nothing, ask nothing, and say nothing. I was like a wet dishrag, without a name really, without an identity. Just hanging around until anyone picked me up, put me in a car, and dropped me off someplace else. The courts would call me different names, and give me different birthdays. I guess no one really knew the true facts. I spent many years in the courtroom with no one telling me anything about myself, no one managing my life, until I was a young adult, and I was released from court wardship. I guess I didn't matter to anyone; no one even cared enough to find out more about me, or so I felt.

Now join me many years later; I'm a trial attorney, litigating a case in court. The courtroom remains cold, distant, and calculated. It smells damp. The male attorneys wear dark colors; the few female attorneys just follow suit, wanting to blend with males. This is tradition, and is supposed to show respect to the judges, my colleagues would say. Some judges ruled that no one could wear colors in their courtroom. If they did, they would be asked to leave. This directive goes against every grain in my soul. As a child, I hated being in a cold and calculated courtroom, and I am not about to tolerate it as an adult. It was not good for me then, and it's not good for my clients, now.

In keeping with my conviction that color was essential in the courtroom, in order to serve the heart of my clients, I showed up to trial with bright red, purple, and turquoise silk blouses. The judges would look at me with discomfort, or perhaps disdain. They didn't dare comment on my attire, as I was a Mexican American, a 'minority woman attorney,' a distinct identity by now. We were in the midst of the Civil Rights Movement, when female attorneys were rare, and female minorities even more so. Many times judges would mistake me for a secretary, or clerk, due to my race, and would ask, "Is the attorney coming?" to which I would respond, "I am counsel, your honor," with a smirk. A judge once sarcastically criticized my purple silk blouse, and said, "Counsel, you certainly add color to the courtroom." I said, "Your Honor was that a racial statement?" The court audience laughed. The judge apologized profusely, and admired my beautiful name instead. He invited me to visit his chambers during recess, to view his Indian artifacts, and assured me he believed in Affirmative Action, a program that is for the enhancement of minorities. After this incident, I was never criticized for wearing color in the courtroom again. Within a few months, many women began to wear bold colors in the courtroom; men later followed. It's now commonplace.

So I stand in trial today, feeling alert, focused, and determined to bring the witness to truth. I will call the witness Sarah. I know Sarah is lying; I wear a street sense of absolute truth that I trust impeccably. I do not know Sarah; she is the plaintiff in the case. I am representing the defendant, and am cross-examining her. I will get to the truth. But I won't destroy her, or damage her, as I have seen many attorneys do, just for the sport of it. This is my last rational thought that day, while litigating the case.

I relied on my street wisdom more than anything else in life. The streets were my home; the only place I really knew. Winning a case took psychology, human relations, legal knowledge, and legal skills, but above all, it took street wisdom. This is where I felt at home, and I trusted this part of me more than anything else. In trial, I used my street wisdom most effectively, and relied heavily on my wisdom that day.

My integrity demanded that I ask questions to the witness that were sincere, authentic, and truth-driven. I could not just lead Sarah into confusion so she would get lost, and answer questions against herself. I had to ask clear, concise, and pure questions. I knew she would step herself into guilt, even with honest questioning. Above all, I held myself in honor, respect, and humility as I cross-examined her.

Sarah sat in the witness stand; I was asking her questions, when suddenly above and behind her there appeared brilliant colors, in all shapes of light; first just angles, then circles, triangles, rectangles, and squares. Hues were just moving through the air. I had never experienced such colors, so bright and vivid. The colored lights began to form into shapes that I recognized (as a child) to be angels. These shapes of light were huge, with big wings loosely defined, somewhat transparent. The Angels began to speak to me, clearly, in English. Telepathically, of course, but I didn't know what that meant at the time. At first I freaked out! Was I going crazy? I was terrified, confused, bewildered, and intrigued. "What on earth?" I thought. I proceeded in trial as though all was normal, as did everyone else, but nothing was normal.

Trial continued as though nothing was happening. I continued also. I wondered what was happening. I felt shocked, and terrified. "Breathe easy, look peaceful," I told myself, even though everything was chaotic. Everyone around me appeared normal for a courtroom scene. The judge, the attorneys, and the jury acted as they usually do in a courtroom. They continued as though nothing different was happening. So I did the same. I listened carefully to the Angels, and somewhat to the judge. "I am losing my mind," I thought. Hearing the Angels was also warm, enticing, persuasive, and somewhat calming. Sometimes one would speak; other times a group. Their voices were one resounding harmonious voice, softly powerful, and with total command.

"Am I having a nervous breakdown? Is this what it feels like?" I thought. There was no one to ask, nowhere to turn. The Angels were sharing nice things, loving things, but why was I hearing them? Was I really going crazy? I didn't know, and the people around me continued to seem so normal. I pretended to be normal too, but I wasn't normal. I felt very lost, wondering what this was all about. If I would just continue acting ok, then trial would continue. I asked questions, Sarah answered. I asked again, she answered. There were objections, argument, motions, everything seemed to flow as usual in trial, yet it wasn't 'usual' at all.

Soon it was more interesting to listen to Angels, and to Spirit, than to court proceedings. They began by giving me information on the case, perhaps to capture and maintain my attention. Facts my investigators had not found were being given to me as if from thin air. My head refused to hear it; my soul knew it was true. Part of me believed the information because I began to use the evidence given by the Angels. The evidence proved true. The witness was soon proving my case, and destroying hers. The other part of me felt I was crazy, "What was I doing, believing and stating facts given to me in my head. How crazy is that?" I thought.

Up until this experience, I had been a very traditional, hard charging attorney, who followed the letter of the law. I had no room for frivolity when it came to social law. Yet, here I was, hearing evidence given to me by Spirit, and using it as though it were true. My soul knew it was true, but my head told me I was insane.

What was even more unsettling was that I was not even religious, much less spiritual. Why me, why now? I was very religious for much of my childhood, placed in many different protestant and catholic foster homes. Each one thought they represented the truth, so I was 'cleansed from sin' often, baptized again and again in each foster home, as the prior home, or institution, had 'poisoned me.' In high school, there were no foster homes available, so the courts placed me in a religious boarding school. I liked it because no one had parents at school, so I wasn't different. I became Religious Editor of the school newspaper, and sang in choirs and small groups at different churches in the community. As a young adult, I believed in God, and religion, but not much longer.

I continued a strong connection to God, but was not aware of it, until my experience in the courtroom. During my first year in college, when I studied comparative religions, I felt very betrayed to know there were many religions, all claiming truth, so I abandoned them all. I never turned back to even view my religious past. None of it made sense. And by the way, I also thought, "Where was God anyway, when I needed him during my scary, lonely childhood?"

Why were Angels appearing to me? I never thought of them. They weren't real to me. Why were they helping me now, in trial? Did they know I was really afraid, very afraid of life, of everything? I had a good front; it could fool anyone, but maybe not the Angels? I seemed friendly, outgoing, and warm, but inside I was crippled. I didn't really know about people.

I had been very abused in many foster homes. Some were very violent, and scary, others distant and disconnected. I didn't feel any of them cared about me. I did survive by being a good babysitter, a good maid, but that was all. As a little child, some homes were so poor; there was little food, no electricity. It was very scary. My clothes were from the Juvenile Hall. It wasn't until after college that I even knew how to buy clothes, or shoes. In Junior High, and beyond, I lived with some very rich, and wealthy families. I was exceptional with children, they loved me a lot, and families valued me because of this. I was a good housekeeper, to the extent that the adults would fire their helpers, so I could clean, and take care of the home. This may have been stupid of me, but it kept the adults away. At the time, I needed this. I felt they weren't safe.

Many times I did not eat with the family. They would eat first. I would get the leftovers, and eat separately. I would clean up for all of them. During holidays, I felt so separate, that I stayed in my room, or arranged to be in the Juvenile Hall. Why me, why Angels? Why could I now see Spirit, without notice? Was I special, or was I weird?

Back in the courtroom, I'm using the Angels' evidence in trial, wondering about all this. My head said it was unreal; my soul said it's pure truth. Towards the closing of my questions, a big ghost appeared to the right side of the witness. It was a big white male form. I could see it clearly. It spoke to me. I almost choked. He placed his hand on the witness' right shoulder, and began to speak. He said, "I am her father, I want her to know I am in court with her today." Yikes! I blinked my eyes many times, trying to stay calm. I didn't even believe in ghosts, and this one was talking to me. I could hear him clearly. He spoke English. Why could I hear him? He looked like the ghosts that I knew of as a child, but they're not real, I thought. I didn't know what was true. Actually I didn't believe in anything. I continued trial in terror; yet intrigued.

I had studied to become an attorney because I believed I could make changes in people's lives, through law. When I was a psychotherapist, things moved too slowly. It could not really change people, because they seemed so attached to their drama.

I was active in community politics at a local, state, and federal level. I participated in and led civil rights activities, and was privileged to meet political leaders at all levels. I had an interest in being the first Hispanic Congresswoman, and was preparing actively for this endeavor. Now what – Angels in the courtroom? After the fear calmed, it was so much more fulfilling to listen to Angels and Spirit, but why, how? Were they real? Why me?

The court recessed for lunch. I sat down at the counsel table, and whispered with senior counsel, Nancy. She was amazed at all the evidence I had gathered, and wondered where I got it. She acknowledged our investigators had not found this data. She was taking notes when she asked, "How did you get the information?"

Nancy was calm, clear, and peaceful. In fact, while investigating her in the past for a political position, the judges I interviewed on her behalf said, "Nancy is the most brilliant mind in the courtroom." Nancy is now my very best friend, a sister I have adopted. She is brilliant, kind, honorable, humble, and unassuming. She is very close to God, and has been my hero for many years. I've had the honor of learning and growing with Nancy. She is very well versed spiritually. Her whole family was involved with metaphysics in one form or another. Though she was senior counsel with me, I didn't even know this part of her. She said I was too uptight and narrow-minded to hear about spirituality at the time. During our legal career, I wondered why she spent so many hours meditating daily, when we could be making money. I guess I wasn't ready to hear her wisdom.

So I answered Nancy's question, "How did you get the evidence?" I said, "Oh, it's written above her head, and there are pictures!" All the specifics were given to me either through conversation, writing, or pictures on the wall. I was actually still trembling at the time we spoke. Nancy just kept taking notes, as though I had said it was a sunny day. She was very calm. She said, "That's great." I said, "Great? Are you crazy? This is not an everyday occurrence! " She said something like, "Well your heart is open, and you are listening carefully, so the universe is giving you information on the case." I had no idea what she was talking about. I remember thinking, "She is crazier than me, don't listen to her..."

You see, I didn't know that Nancy had been a meditator for numerous years. She practiced Transcendental Meditation for many years before she met me. Seeing and talking to Spirit was a familiar conversation to her. She said I was in touch with the universe, so I was getting information on others. Could that be true? What did she mean? She validated all that had happened, by staying very still, and just knowing. "She must be from a different planet", I thought. I didn't understand what was happening, but I was determined to find out, whatever it took. This was my Spiritual Awakening, and an awesome one at that! I just didn't know what it was.

During court recess, we went to lunch at a nice restaurant near the bay that attorneys and other business people frequented. It was beautiful, very light, with pretty colors, and many windows. As I walked in, it felt crowded, but I quickly spotted Sarah, the witness I had cross-examined in court, at a table with a friend. I didn't recognize her friend, but I could see it was not her lawyer. I was even more determined to get to the truth about Spirit. Perhaps this woman brought the Angels, the Spirit with her? What did she know about all this? I didn't even know what questions to ask, or how to ask. I said to my partner, "I'm going to say hello to the witness." She cautioned me, reminding me of our code that one side cannot speak to the opposing side's client. I was not about to risk not getting information I needed about the profound Spiritual experience in court that day. I said something like, "Oh, I'm just going to say hello. I was very assertive with her during cross-examination, so I just want to greet her..." and I took off. I was determined to learn what I could about the incident.

I approached Sarah's table at lunch. She saw me coming, and looked down. She seemed timid, and scared. I had asked penetrating questions, and there was reason for her to be afraid. I moved softly close to her, and a bit silenced in energy. She was eating, but paused. She was dressed very professionally, with light colors. Her eyes remained downcast. I asked, "How are you?" She said, "I'm ok," rather shyly. It was a low, dull voice. I could barely hear her. "Are you close to your father?" I asked. She seemed taken aback, and very sensitive to the question. Why would I be asking about her father, whom I knew nothing about? She didn't understand, nor did I. It just came out, I suppose because I saw him as a ghost. Tears came to her eyes, and she said, "Yes, we were very close, all my life. He died just one month ago; I miss him a lot, all the time. " I replied, "He wants you to know he was in court with you today," to which she responded, "I know, I felt him touch my shoulder." She pointed to her right shoulder, which was the shoulder I had seen him touch. Nothing else mattered. This was the direct evidence I needed to know there was some truth to what had just happened in the courtroom, and I was about finding out what it was.

This profound Spiritual experience was the turning point to my whole life. It was instant! The Angels knew, God knew, I needed direct evidence that what I was seeing and hearing in court was true, nothing more – nothing less. My whole world collapsed right in front of me. Everything I knew was not true. My whole life was a lie. There were reasons for my being that were far beyond anything I could imagine. There was something more, something greater than what I had ever been exposed to. Nothing made sense. There was Spirit, there was God, there were Angels, and they were true. This invalidated all of my life, my identity, my story, my beliefs; they were all out the window. None of that made any sense. My destiny had taken over. My Heart, Soul and Spirit had taken over. I thought, "I'm not a therapist, I'm not a lawyer, and I'm not a politician. Nothing's true. What now?"

Now let me tell you why I told you that the Angels and Spirit gave me evidence in my case. This was only to get my attention, and keep it. What was most magnificent was what else they shared. During the litigation, while completely focused on the case, I was also receiving very powerful, magnificent Universal Truths. I did not know at the time that I was being given the Deepest and Highest Universal Teachings by Spiritual Masters themselves. This sharing gave me clear guidance in my life, clear direction. I no longer question anything. I have full faith in the Universe, in God. I now know Love, Peace, Joy, and Abundance in my daily life. I know it's my very essence, my Divine Essence. It comes easily and graciously. I am very committed and devoted to giving you some of this wisdom, as I have received it freely, and freely I will give. Some of the incredible wisdom went something like this:

We know you have suffered a traumatic childhood. Your perceptions and interpretations of this are hurting you now. It is your limited beliefs and perceptions that hold you back, and do not allow a loving, and abundant life. Change your beliefs, your choices, and your behavior, and you will elevate your life tremendously. We are here to remind you that you are a Divine Being, whose True Essence is Divine Love, Peace, and Joy. It is not intended that you, or anyone, should continue to suffer, and distance yourself. Your time on earth is to be Joyful, peaceful, and giving. In the human experience, because you have separated yourself from the whole, you will experience separation within you, and outside of you. But this is an illusion. The Truth is that you are Whole, one with the Infinite Intelligence of the Universe. You are not to attach to separation of any kind, such as judging yourself, blaming yourself, or blaming others. You are in the world, but not of the world. Connect again with Universal Intelligence, and remember who you truly are. You are just remembering, this is not new to you. You have walked a Spiritual path many times before.

Remember your True Essence of Unconditional Love. Life is intended to be peaceful and joyful, it is only your choices that make it difficult. Your soul is of Love Divine, as it is in Union of Spirit. You are not the beliefs you have created about you, because of your circumstances. This is only your ego, which is separation. Your ego holds you separate in personality, but your soul knows Union, Oneness, and a deep connection with Source. In wholeness, you are perfect as you are. You need not do anything, nor be anything to be loved. You are love, Love Divine. Love is the State of Being, and is nothing you can strive for. It is not a feeling that comes and goes, but is your state, which is everlasting and eternal. You need only tap into it.

Your soul chose the life you have lived on earth, and your soul can return you to Spirit, or Love Divine, while walking the earth. You cannot reach this level of bliss and wisdom through your head, or your ego. Your ego is based on fear, lack, and survival. It separates you from God. You can only Remember and Realize Divine Truth through your Heart, Soul and Spirit. No one has done anything to hurt you. It's only your interpretation, and perceptions, and they are based on your fears. People were just living their life, and you misinterpreted it. Now you build your life on the mistrust, anger, and fear that you learned and adopted through others.

When you come from Love Divine, you will know that you choose all your experiences, and only you can change them. For now, choose your thoughts wisely. Soon your thoughts will subside, and become irrelevant. Silence will overtake you as you enter your Divine Essence. Select carefully the feelings you will focus on, for they are of this dimension, and support you to not believe in your Divinity and Wholeness. Only allow feelings that support your ultimate vision of Love and Freedom. Do not build your life on negative feelings, for they come and go, and your house will fall. Do not focus on feelings or thoughts that hurt you, for you will attract more of the same. This is the Universal Law: Whatever you believe you must manifest. Set your heights on the Love of God, the love of mankind. Lift yourself and all those around you with this light of Universal Truth, and you will free you, and many others.

You have a deep connection with the Spiritual Master, Joshua bar Joseph, or Jesus, as you know Him in the west. He came to earth to teach Unconditional Love, but the masses misinterpreted His work, and were not ready for His pure teachings of Love. He is one of your Spirit Guides, and continues to work closely with you.

The Truth is very simple and clear. Spiritual Masters who have walked before you have brought this simple message to earth, and those who are ready will hear it. You and others will elevate the vibrations of the planet by sharing these Universal Truths.

During this spiritual delivery, my head was going berserk; my soul was still and deep. Part of me thought, "What a joke, why me? Do you know whom you're talking to? Why now? Where were you when I needed you?" I was against traditional religion by the time of this sighting, and never even entertained the idea of God. What is this all about? But so much of what they said was so beautiful, so powerful, so freeing. It felt true, but I wasn't sure why. They had given me evidence on the court case that was true, and effective. I was a bit angry that they would impose these truths at this stage in my life. "What on earth was I to do with this?" If it was true, it turned my whole world upside down.

The Angels and Spirit Guides flooded my life daily with support, guidance, and awesome Universal Wisdom. I could see them, feel them, hear them, and interact with them. Soon, I had no other interest. I'd spend hours, days, nights, and weeks at a time meditating, listening to, and incorporating these truths. At times I would meditate all day, and some nights. I only wanted direction from God on how to know and live these Universal Truths. This connection with Spirit had a profound impact on my life. My whole life shifted in a big way. I no longer wanted anything to do with Social Law, only Sacred Law. My interest in law and politics disappeared. My focus in the material world quieted. I now live in Love, Peace, and Knowing each day. Joy and Freedom prevail in my life. Spirit continues to be very evident in my everyday life.

Soon thereafter, the Spirit realm asked me to share this information with the world when I felt centered. This I share with you. Twelve very dynamic teachings that helped me immediately and I know will support you, are:

1. *Love and Accept* yourself fully and completely, no matter what.

2. Always *remember* that you are *One with God, the Universe.*

3. Know that you are *Divine Love, a Child of God.* His Love flows through you with every breath you take.

4. Wake up every morning, and go to bed every night, in *Gratitude* for who you are, and what you have created up to now. This opens the portals to *Abundance.*

5. You are not separate. Separation is an illusion. We are all connected, *Heart, Soul, and Spirit*

6. Do not walk alone. It was intended that we help each other return to our *Divine Source*, while on earth. Surround yourself with good support from people that are in harmony with you, and your vision.

7. Drop immediately any beliefs, thoughts, feelings, and actions, that do not support your highest good. Do not entertain for one minute that you are not good enough, smart enough, fast enough, etc. These beliefs you have adopted from others.

8. You are one with *Infinite Intelligence*, and you can manifest whatever you desire when you see yourself in the *light of Universal Intelligence.* The Universe is yours for the asking. "*...Ask and you will receive...*" *Infinite Possibilities* are yours when you wear *Divine Love.* In this state you can create whatever you desire.

9. Reach for the sky to create and attract a magnificent life! Never hold yourself back; never undermine yourself.

10. Give to others, as freely as you have been given to, for in the giving is receiving. When you're tired of giving, give again.

11. What is most valued in life is what you cannot pay for. Take in the magnificence of the Universe, honor it, appreciate it, and be humbled by it.

12. You came to earth for one reason, and one reason only. That is to *return to Unconditional Love, Divine Love*, while walking in physical limitation. Unless your journey includes this evolution, you will never be fulfilled.

I began to share these *Divine Truths*, and many others, to whomever would listen. Soon the groups got bigger and bigger, and we finally created The S.O.U.L. Institute Inc., in California, for the purpose of sharing with others these wonderful Universal Principles, and guiding them to transform their lives to *Love, Peace, Joy, Freedom, and Abundance* in every way. We have been sharing these teachings for over 20 years, and have touched many souls from all over the world, and in many walks of life. We have fulfilled our **Destiny** by sharing these *Universal Principles* with you. We invite you to fulfill yours.

May God continue to Bless You, as you continue to bless others.

We can be reached at: S.O.U.L. Institute Inc. www.soulinstitute.com. Info@soulinstitute.com (877) For My Soul = (877) 469 – 7685

About Esperanza

Esperanza Universal is the Co-Creator and CEO of the S.O.U.L. Institute, Inc., in San Diego, CA, where she teaches people how to transform their lives with a Simple and Powerful System, based on Spiritual Laws. Esperanza started the S.O.U.L. Institute after a profound Spiritual experience while litigating a case in court. Before becoming an attorney, Esperanza was a psychotherapist, a probation officer, an Equal Employment Opportunity Officer, and worked in the Juvenile Justice System. She was active in civic activities and community politics. Esperanza's interest was to become the first Hispanic Congresswoman. As an attorney, Esperanza was a fiery advocate for her clients, and was known as a "Tiger" in the courtroom. Esperanza then founded the S.O.U.L. Institute Inc., where she teaches people how to remove obstacles from their life, and how to create the life they truly desire.

A CELEBRATION OF LIFE

BY KEVIN SMITH

No one cheerfully attends a funeral. In fact, the only reason I agreed to come to this one was to appear supportive in my budding, new relationship. I had said, "Yes," to my friend, presuming it would be just another burial. Funny enough, the end of one life ended up being the beginning of another. Without even knowing it, celebrating the life of someone I didn't know would have a profound effect on my future.

On that gray January day in Oregon, the frost-covered leaves crackled underfoot as my new partner and I approached the chapel full of despondent funeral-goers. Each one had his or her own reason for being there; none as disconnected as mine. They were all strangers to me, and I to them. If the number of mourners and their emotional responses could be factored into a person's worth, this was a highly valued woman.

While being cordially introduced, I listened to conversations, piecing together the deceased had been in her 50's, just a few years older than I was at the time of her death. She died unexpectedly, on the operating table during a routine surgery.

When the music began to play, the clusters of guests disbanded and folded themselves quietly into their seats. I surveyed the room, expecting the attendees to be clad in black with oversized sunglasses to hide their pain from the outside world – but they weren't. They seemed to be happy, almost celebrating the occasion. I settled in alongside my new partner at the back of the chapel, doing my best to appear as someone who wanted to be there, despite thinking about how much I really didn't. Attending a funeral with no real connection to the deceased is a unique experience. You are like a sponge or a mirror, simply absorbing the feelings of others and doing your best to reflect similar sentiments, whether you feel them or not.

A woman dressed in a purple business suit stepped onto the stage and welcomed us to Ginger's celebration of life. The joyful smile that spread across her face caught me off-guard.

Aren't funerals supposed to be sad affairs? I thought to myself.

She continued, confidently gripping the microphone, "I'd like to share a few words about the way our beloved lived her life, and the good we can harvest from her remarkable example."

Pictures of happy people, hugging and smiling, enjoying life together, flashed up on a screen behind the speaker's head. A kinship began to develop between the deceased and me. I related to her because I lived a happy life as well. I had a well-paying job, I saved plenty for my retirement, I owned a beautiful home in one of the best neighborhoods in Houston, Texas, and I surrounded myself with wonderful friends and family. I was in control of my life.

"The first time I met Ginger," the speaker said, "a friend had brought her to the Church of New Thought, where I preached in Scholls, Oregon. After her husband lost his job, her family offered them and their two daughters a place back 'home', on the farm where she had been raised. They were given some breathing room to rebuild their lives. At church, much of the information I taught was new to her. I shared with her she was in control of her own destiny. The idea that she could design her own life was a new concept for her. I wasn't surprised when she pulled me aside one Sunday, and asked me an interesting question, "Could I change my name?"

"Of course you can. You are the master of your life. You can do whatever you choose," I replied. So, as an adult, she renamed herself 'Ginger', since she never particularly cared for her birth name. This one decision empowered her and profoundly changed her entire life.

This was the first time I ever heard of a 'normal' person changing their name. I knew that criminals took on aliases and new names, but it was only because they had something to hide. I thought: *If someone could change something as important as their name, then perhaps I could make some changes to my life, too.* This was new territory for me, but the idea of doing something wild, liberated me, and left me feeling full of motivation and inspiration.

The speaker continued on, "Ginger and I became close as time went on. She was always cheerful with an infectious laugh." I watched as the audience bobbed their heads in agreement and chuckled knowingly. "Frankly, I wanted to be around her giving spirit as much as I could, so I offered her a job as my personal assistant. One could only hope to be as happy as Ginger was while she was with us," she said, comfortably walking from one side of the stage to the other.

Am I happy? I wondered. I was proud of my illustrious 27-year finance career in corporate America. But in the end, pride and happiness are two completely separate things. I could be proud but still unhappy. Many people are. Honestly, my job didn't fulfill me. I managed to tolerate it by taking the inner-position that the company would fold if I weren't there grinding it out every day. I had grown tired of the office politics and the endless piles of work and responsibility. I felt as if I was on an island, always looking for a lifeboat of purpose that would never appear. Something had to change, and I knew it. But what? How? I was so ingrained in my life that I felt there was no way out. Change seemed just as scary as the status quo – or so I thought.

"Later in life, Ginger found that her special purpose was being of service to others. She gave with passion her time, her money, and herself. Everyone around her was happy because she was happy. She had found her purpose. Every one of you is here today because she found her special purpose. Ginger mattered," she said, wandering through the crowd.

As she passed by, each person in the audience pivoted in their seats to follow her with his or her eyes. I noticed they were all fully engaged, hanging on her every last word as if she was narrating a dramatic mystery. This woman spoke with polish and poise. She was an amazing storyteller who shared a wonderful tale of life and meaning.

At this point, she invited anyone in the crowd to stand and say a few words in memory of the deceased. One after the other, friends, family, co-workers, and neighbors stood and told stories about how Ginger had changed their lives. I was suddenly seized by the thought: *What are people going to say about me at my funeral?* My initial reaction was that I would be staring down from above and hearing, time and time again, "Oh, that guy worked so hard."

I didn't want to be known only as a hard worker! I wanted my funeral attendees to clearly be able to answer the question: What value did I add to their lives? I wondered, *does my life as a hard worker even matter?* I wanted to do more, give more, live more like Ginger.

After all the attendees concluded their comments, the speaker brought the ceremony to a close.

She said, "Spend some time asking yourself, 'who am I and why am I here?' If you do, you will discover that you have infinite potential. Ginger lived and died without regret, because she found her passion and her purpose, and you can, too."

As I surveyed the room, I noted most of the congregation in tears. I had listened intently, and I found tears streaming down my cheeks as well. It was as if her words had been directed at me. Somehow, Ginger had reached through the veil of death to get my attention in life. I was shocked into complete alertness when the final question came: "What special purpose does life have for you?"

I hung my head and thought about why, in nearly three decades as a financial executive, nobody had ever asked me any questions like these. During my career, I had played the game right and worked my way up the ranks to become a successful CFO. I was responsible for the financial management of a division in one of the largest companies in the United States – and I was miserable in the process. I couldn't help but survey my life and think, *how much longer am I going to allow myself to be unhappy in this unfulfilling executive job?*

The speaker took a seat next to the grieving family, but nobody in the audience moved. I assume they were all reflecting on their own lives, just like I. During the eulogy, her words had struck a chord in me, and rattled my mortality cage. Life was short and my time was running out. *Is it too late to make changes?*

Bending to my right, I asked the person seated next to me, "Who is she?"

"Oh, that's Mary Morrissey – she's an internationally-renowned personal development coach and thought leader." I had never heard of her before, but I decided I would research her when I got home.

By the time the funeral was over and the mourners had left, I had made the decision to leave my job. I concluded that I deserved to live a more fulfilling life. Without having any idea what that meant, my decision to celebrate life was made that day. I left my reputable job just a few months later. With the good fortune of retiring early, I was finally free from the rat race, with time to pursue a more gratifying life.

In our culture, the definition of retirement generally means living a life of leisure – and I took full advantage. My days were soon filled with travel, reading, watching television, surfing the Internet, and working out – all the things I put off because of my strenuous job. I succumbed to the great retirement myth, and soon was looking around and asking myself, "What is the point of all this?" I had lost sight of the reason for my early retirement in the first place. I forgot about what Mary had said at Ginger's funeral. I retired, but for all the wrong reasons. Even in retirement, my passion remained hidden. Where was my passion?

To ward off the boredom, I decided to get involved in community service. I fed the homeless, sat on company boards, and helped award scholarships to students at a local university. My days were soon filled with volunteering, but after each event, I still felt hollowness in the pit of my stomach. The more things changed, the more they seemed to stay the same. Although I was helping people who had found purpose in their lives by starting their own charities, where was mine?

During this blind journey, a dear friend invited me to go with her to a health spa in Northern Mexico. It was one where only healthy food choices found their way onto the menu. With all the exercise options offered, I was certain to lose some extra weight and tone up. Every morning, a brave few chose to hike up to the top of a mountain and watch the sunrise. We marveled at how the sun rose behind us and cast its rays over our heads, dancing on the waves of the distant Pacific Ocean.

During the hike back, I struck up a conversation with a woman named Nancy. We really hit it off, and shared with one another all the things that were going on in our lives. I told her I had retired early, but still hadn't found anything I really wanted to do – I hadn't yet found my passion. She said something that profoundly impacted me, "Passion never retires." This struck a chord, and suddenly, I had an idea.

I couldn't get back to my room fast enough to start work on my new idea. I wanted to research how I could find my purpose, and how I could help others find theirs. I realized that helping other people was my true calling. That was the puzzle piece I had been looking for all along. The greatest excitement and the biggest rewards come in the form of helping another person find his or her roadmap to success. All the greats discuss the importance of finding what makes your heart sing. Money is then an ancillary result of living your passion. I felt as if I finally found it.

I had met many retired people over the course of my travels. A lot of them were older people who do their shopping in the middle of the day or go to the pool right after normal lunch hours to avoid dealing with the masses. Many of them, like me, saved for retirement. But like me, they also hadn't planned on how they would spend their time. Even though they weren't working, they hadn't found their purpose, and passion never retires.

That phrase returned to me over and over again. I thought about it all the time. I decided to use it as my company's name. *Passion Never Retires* – from La-Z-Boy to living the life of your dreams. My target market are retirees who still want to contribute to others and leave their mark on this world, but don't know how to do so. While hiking in Northern Mexico with Nancy, I realized I could help guide other people to find their true passion.

My work has involved the creation of an online program to help people figure out what it is they want to do. Nothing could give me greater joy than helping retirees avoid the pitfalls I found for myself after my own retirement. From this, I was able take actual success stories of students and use those in my practice. Through these lessons, my ultimate goal and desire is to help people live a more fulfilling and satisfying life on their own terms. I quit a completely safe and secure job to live life in a manner I deemed more fulfilling and purposeful. It wasn't easy, however, deep down in my heart I knew it was necessary.

After working on my idea for a while, I had the web address and much of the curriculum already written. I was turning my vision into a reality, but the one thing that was missing was a coaching component to my business, a framework with which I would guide my students. If I intended to be a life coach, I wanted to learn from someone who already had a successful process in place.

When a friend recommended I enroll and become certified in Mary Morrissey's Dreambuilder coaching program, I just about fell out of my chair. How ironic that her name entered my life again after all those years ago, when I first met her at a funeral for a woman I didn't even know. It was at that funeral that Mary suggested I pursue my passion, and live a life like Ginger had lived.

Before long I was participating in Mary Morrissey's Dreambuilder Live event not only as an attendee, but also as a certified Dreambuilder life coach. As you can imagine, it was wonderful to have the opportunity to share with her the impact she had on me. The eulogy she gave celebrating her friend's life completely changed the course of my life. On that day, I know her goal was to celebrate life, but unintentionally, she changed at least one. I now dream of locking arms with Mary and sharing the stage to help a long-neglected demographic: retirees who think it's too late for them to live a life filled with meaning and purpose. Together we can show them that a world of possibilities awaits.

My experience is a perfect example of why it is never too late. I am now a retired man who has discovered that my destiny is to help others find whatever it is that makes them happy and pursue it. It doesn't matter that someone didn't put a plan in place earlier to plot out the course of his or her own journey. There is no time like the present, and it is never too late to infuse purpose into your life. If I can help prevent just one person from avoiding the mistakes I made, it will have all been worth it.

Time is not a renewable resource – we only get a limited amount of it. We can't get any wasted time back. We really have no idea as to how much time we get in the first place. Contrast that with money, which is infinite, renewable, and available. Strangely enough, people spend their entire lives financially planning for their retirement, but then fail to purposefully plan for their future. They find themselves rich in wealth, but poor in life.

Now, I must ask you, "What special purpose does life hold for you?" Take some time to think about that question – really think hard. When you let your mind wander and allow yourself to dream, you will discover something about which you are passionate. It may be something you've put off doing because of school, or your career, or your family, or your kids – let's face it, life probably got in the way. That is the norm for most of us, but we are all in charge of our own **destinies**. Realize though, it is never too late to do something new – to pursue your passion. If you discover what your special purpose is, you, my friend, will hold the keys to the kingdom.

Life is short. The clock is ticking. Do you hear it? Are you even listening? The gift of retirement is a gift of time – time to do what couldn't be done, time to make the most of your life, and time to wake up each day filled with passion and purpose. You can move the needle towards the direction of your dreams. We all have the heart of a person like Ginger within us. We are born to serve, and to help one another progress and evolve in life. Don't wait until your own funeral to ask the question: *Did I do enough?* I was one of the lucky ones. For me, the celebration of one life fueled the rebirth of another. John Maxwell said, "Every person has a longing to be significant, to make a contribution, to be a part of something noble and purposeful."

Purpose is our **destiny**. Are you heading in the right direction?

About Kevin

Kevin Smith, graduated from The Ohio State University with a Bachelor of Science in Business Administration. After a long and illustrious career, holding leadership roles within the Finance team of Cardinal Health, one of the top 20 largest companies within the Fortune 500, he had the good fortune of retiring after almost 28 years with the company at the relatively early age of 51. After a wake-up call in which he found a strong desire to align his passion and values with a "purpose"; he began to work with organizations and individuals, helping them to build their dreams, accelerate their results, and create richer, more fulfilling lives under his banner Passion Never Retires.

WHAT DO YOU REALLY WANT TO DO?

By Lorrie Pande

It was April of 2016 and I was on my way to the airport from Charlotte to Toronto for the Matrixx Event. Everything flowed. On a beautiful spring day with a smooth ride to the airport and no wait at security I got to the gate within plenty of time. I have always been aware of the number 11 because for me, this number pops up when things are feeling right. Whenever I see this number I feel like I am in alignment. The gate for my airplane was Gate 11, but I was not surprised because I had a very strong feeling I was on my path toward my destiny. My First Class seat was purchased with an old credit card I found that happened to have just enough points for the upgrade. With no one sitting next to me, I called my two front seats, number 11. It was going to be that kind of day!

With a beautiful landing and a shuttle to the Westin Prince Hotel where I would spend six glorious days of learning about the Power of Attraction, my valet ushered me straight to the front desk. As I checked in, I said to the clerk, "I hope my room number has an 11 in it because that's my lucky number." At the very same moment, he handed my room key to me and said, "My dear, you've got your number." I looked at the key and I was astonished! I had been given Room 1111! "Who's writing this, I thought to myself?" How many 11's can I get in one day? It felt like I was floating down a river of continuous alignment toward the Proctor Gallagher Matrixx Event.

I was beginning to suspect I was going to get more out of this week than I had planned. I would get the help I needed to enhance my business in order to make a bigger profit, and become more successful. Now if you go to the Matrixx Event and you think that's what you are going to get, think again! You have no idea what is going to happen, but expect something way beyond what you have ever dreamed.

Day one was wonderful! Sitting at round tables among eighty people searching for their goals was the best kind of learning I could possibly imagine. The lecture series with Bob Proctor and Sandy Gallagher was fresh and exciting and the feeling in the room felt all around awesome. It was during a break when I got the chance to speak with Bob's partner, Sandy. She asked me this one very simple question, "What do you really want to do, Lorrie?"

Without responding immediately, my internal dialogue began. I was speechless, dumbfounded, hesitant. But when am I ever at a loss for words? Think quickly. Wait a minute, who asks this question? What do I want to do? Come on that should be easy. She wants to know? Just talk. Talk about why you came, what you came for, why you're here…

I told her about my online antique business, and how I wanted to increase my sales with an e-commerce website, since I currently sold my items as a dealer on a site in New York. I wanted my business to expand beyond online sales, by providing a service of staging sets and props for the film industry. I wanted to offer it to photographers and filmmakers for photo shoots with my furniture collection from around the globe. I thought this was a really cool idea and needed assistance. This was my purpose for attending the Matrixx Event. But all of that was just "Blah, blah, blah," since Sandy actually wanted to hear something more convincing. Sandy replied, "Nah, that's not it. What do you really want to do? Lorrie, what do you really, really want to do?"

I had stood in line for a while to see Sandy and was actually accused of cutting in line by someone. I defended myself and said I couldn't be seen behind a very tall man, and I really hadn't cut in line at all. Had I not been politely persistent, I might have missed my chance to speak with Sandy. I might have lost what was about to take place. I might have missed a focal point moment. That moment that would take me back to what I really wanted to do thirty years ago, something deep that had been buried inside me. It was less than a five minute conversation that would change my destiny and almost everything I do and the way I do it.

I imagined when I met Sandy and shared my idea, she would introduce me to options that would help me with my business goals. To my surprise she had no interest in listening to me talk about my business. Instead, she looked at me and asked me in the most serious way, as if I hadn't been honest with her, "Lorrie, what do you really want to do?" This question puzzled me at first. I had to accept the possibility that she didn't hear me, or she didn't think that my idea was a good one. In any other circumstance I might have defended myself, but I had to let go of that thought and follow her lead or she might not want to waste her time waiting for me to be indecisive.

What I was about to say would erupt through countless layers of paradigms that had cloaked my dreams in blankets of denial. The words came from deep within my solar plexus and rolled off my tongue as they spewed out into the ethers like a Shakespearean Insult. "I WANT TO DIRECT A BROADWAY MUSICAL," I said as if I was shouting.

Her immediate response was, "That's it! That's it right there, that is exactly what you have to do, and that is what you truly want."

"Really? Really, that's it?" I said in disbelief.

Oh she believes me? I'm worthy of that? Well, why shouldn't I be? I directed musicals for thirty years, and really good ones too – but just not on Broadway. Feeling sick and disoriented, I thought, "How in the heck am I going to do that? This isn't what I came here for at all," I thought to myself, suddenly feeling like I just left my comfort zone. Little did I know then, that this was something big for me! Could this be my destiny?

I said, "But how do you know that?" I implored as if I needed to be convinced.

Sandy continued. "Because of the glow around you. Your posture changed, your color changed, everything about you changed when you said you wanted to direct a Broadway Musical. That's it, that's what you want to do and that's what you have to do." And she was off to answer the next person's question.

Within seconds, a ray of thoughts flooded my mind – what just happened? Where am I? Now what? Who can I tell, I don't know anyone here yet. Call my friends? Nope. No one's going to believe this. Nobody except the people in this room. Little did I know that very soon I would meet my Master Mind Group and have the chance to share my ideas. After that amazing experience, I knew something great was about to happen. As I would later come to hear Bob Proctor say in a Paradigm Shift Seminar, "And the truth burst upon us like a revelation!" It was exactly that for me at that moment, a huge revelation!

Having directed theatre for most of my life, I knew I could do this. I could write the play and all the songs too; however, I had no idea how I would get to that place of winning a Tony Award. How was I going to do this? Later I would hear this supporting quote from Bob Proctor, "You'll attract all things requisite for the fulfillment of the image by the harmonious vibration of Law of Attraction."

By day two I made friends with the people that would form my Master Mind Group. We were a most unlikely team: a Swedish Lady Obstetrician, a male Aeronautical Engineer from Austria, a Network Marketer and Creative Business woman from Mississippi and me… a retired Musical Theatre Director and Estate Furniture Entrepreneur.

That same day head-shot photographer, Peter Hurley presented his Ted Talks video and I recognized one of my students in the featured shot. It was lovely to connect with Peter and to learn what a talented, kind and high frequency individual he was. For those of you who have come to know him, I have one thing to say: "SHABANG!" Peter's expletive!

Across the crisp white round tables in the Convention Hall, we studied the Matrixx Program with Bob and Sandy by day and by night our team laughed and dined together while sharing our ideas with each other. After my meeting with Sandy I was so relieved to have made friends with people I could trust to share my new goal. With their support, I felt invincible. This journey would take me into another dimension of study which would become the direction for my life purpose. Who knew you could find a life purpose later in life? Age hang up is a paradigm as I have come to learn and it simply does not matter because your Destiny has no limitations!

On the fifth day we presented our goals to all the participants in the room. We travelled from table to table pitching our dreams in a game called SNAP! Participants would place a card in your bag and at the end of the session we would go home with little bags of connections. Part of this exercise involved reaching out to the person on the card to see how we could support each other through future networking.

I was amazed to see a room full of eighty highly successful people: writing, re-writing, scribbling, and changing again and again one simple paragraph that said – "I am so happy and grateful now that I am…" This, all in answer to the same question Sandy Gallagher had asked me earlier, "What do you really want to do?"

The last day of the Matrixx Event was spent at Bob Proctor's house in Toronto. It was great to see Bob's library and recording studio where he broadcasts his Inner Circle Sessions through Skype. He opened his home to us as we enjoyed the delicious banquet of food, wine and good company. Our group, having spent only six days together had gotten to know each other at our deepest levels of desire – to live the life of our dreams. Many of us had become family and if nothing less, a great support system for each other.

As I traveled home, I was on Cloud Nine! I couldn't wait to begin writing my Broadway Musical and I knew exactly what the subject would be!

It was springtime in Asheville when I began writing. I drove through the Biltmore Forest for inspiration and immersed myself in the woody fragrance of rain forest trees, the flowering Rhododendrons and Azaleas. The variety of songbirds in colors of red, blue and yellow darting through the forest is never more alive than in springtime. It was during one of my drives that I saw a dream house for sale in the Biltmore Forest and fell head over heels in love with it. It was a big beautiful 1920s French provincial home with grand English gardens lined with Cypress trees and a circular pea gravel drive with a fountain in the center. I did not have the courage to make an offer because at the time I did not "feel worthy"… yet during this entire process everything began to flow. I would drive through the forest while pulling over to write lyrics as ideas came to mind. I did this all of spring and half of summer. In fact, I wrote nine songs in about two months' time, while imagining I lived in that house, as I progressed with my Broadway Musical.

It was that dream house which helped me believe I was worthy. Within the beautiful setting, the focus of my desire put me in the frequency to write my play. I truly believed I deserved to live in a "prosperous environment in order to use my gift," as Bob taught us. With the support of the Inner Circle and my Master Mind group, I was encouraged and empowered to write. The more I studied the easier the writing became, and most of the time it flowed. I thought I had fallen in love with the house, but I fell in love with the dream. Later I would learn from Bob Proctor, "It's not what you have, it's what you do."

One morning, I woke up to a windy day with chimes blowing. I ran to get my tiny glockenspiel while hammering out the notes for a ballad about the wind, which was to become one of the most important songs in the musical.

In an email, I received an invitation from Bob Proctor to attend an event in August at the Mauna Lani Resort in Kona Hawaii, called 1%. I decided almost immediately to attend and made the necessary arrangements. "The universe responds to speed," I heard Bob say in my mind. I was now going to Hawaii in August where I knew I would gain further momentum for my play.

Before leaving for Hawaii, I made the decision to sign contracts to rent a very large Broadway size theatre in which to workshop ACT I, upon my return. This commitment, I thought would force me to write the play or at least have it far enough along so that I could write in between the workshops and have a finished ACT I by the end of our workshop week.

Hawaii was magical! I swam, I wrote, I studied, and connected with people with whom I shared my goals. This event was where the 'C' Goal became clear to me. An A Goal is something you know you can do. A B Goal is something you think you can do but a C Goal is something far out of your grasp and not many people get there! Not because they can't but because they gave up.

We each had our forty-five minutes on stage with Bob. The time with him was "high frequency." I handed him a water bottle and told him it was my Tony Award but I didn't have it yet. He said, "Oh yes you do, you already do!" He was referring to the C Goal. You imagine your goal is in the present and you have already attained it by envisioning it and writing it down every single day. It was wonderful to hear Bob get excited about my idea and have him relate it to the other students. He even made some connections for me with the professionals that were there to help us. He touched on self-image quite a bit and I have since come to understand that when you become one with your goal, you are using your gift and your self-image will line right up. 1% was everything that I had hoped for and more.

Ocean view rooms and early morning breakfasts with a small group of students followed by hours of study together lead by Bob, filled the days while seaside lunches, sunset dinners and a Catamaran adventure delightfully consumed the remaining hours. At one point we were situated on the water exactly between a full moon over a volcano to the east and the sun setting into the sea followed by the green flash in the west. Our boat was smack dab in the middle and it was divine!

When I returned from 1%, I went straight into auditions for my play. A company of eight "perfect" people showed up and I had exactly what I needed to create ACT I. I took a day off for my birthday and on Labor Day weekend, I wrote enough of the play to get started. We had the melodies recorded that I had written from my head, a skin drum and one lone glockenspiel for accompaniment. We got through the first three scenes, and then I began reading to the cast while they improvised. By night, I wrote about the improvisation giving lines to all of the characters and each day they would act out their new scripts. Within four days, an entire ACT had been created and even videotaped.

Shortly after the workshop, I received a letter from the administrative offices of the "powers that be" confirming permission with free artistic license to produce my musical based on the historical character in the play. This was amazing news. It was the affirmation that I was on the right path... my **destiny**, the path of my desire in answer to Sandy's question, "What do you really want to do?"

"I WANT TO DIRECT A BROADWAY MUSICAL, Sandy Gallagher! Thanks very much for asking!"

And now I ask you reader to ask yourself the question – "What do you really want to do?" It's never too late and it's never too soon! You may not know the answer right away, but do yourself a favor and take the time to figure it out. Begin your search, make a decision, write it down, over and over until you know it's what you want and then envision it. See it as if it has already happened and don't lose sight of that goal!

You too can discover your... destiny!

ABOUT LORRIE

Originally from the Chicago area, Lorrie began studying acting at the early age of ten. Lorrie acted in plays and majored in Theatre and Dance at Stephens College where she earned her BFA. In 1979, she began her own children's theatre in Evanston, where she also managed young people in Films & Commercials as well as worked on a Children's Radio Show for WBEZ. In 1985, she moved to Florida with her husband and two daughters. Lorrie was also an events coordinator for her father's company and directed the entertainment at The grand Ole Opry, The Fairmont in New Orleans, and the Hotel Del Coronado to name a few. She got her MA at Northwestern University in the year 2001 and continued teaching Theatre, Film and TV to Children. She wrote curriculums for schools while developing her teaching method from decades of teaching experience before she retired and opened her business called Treasure Keepers in Asheville. Treasure Keepers is now what Lorrie calls an MSI (Multiple Source of Income), an online antique shop where people can make purchases from her estate collections. She found Bob Proctor on a Live Stream Event in the fall of 2015 and began studying with Inner Circle, Matrixx and attended 1% in Hawaii. She thanks Bob Proctor and Sandy Gallagher for bringing her back to theatre to find her true Destiny as she writes and directs her Broadway Musicals!

BEING A TRANSFORMATIONALIST

BY JAY BILLIG

My mother had sixteen pregnancies, thirteen of which made it to full term and birth. Of those thirteen, the split was ten boys and three girls. It is a pretty safe bet that with that many children there is some deep faith going on or at least guiding principles that favor unhindered procreation. In our case, we were raised Catholic. Now, there are plenty of families in Catholic faith communities who are lukewarm about it and attend only for major holidays, weddings and funerals. We were on the opposite end of the spectrum.

We went to church every week and my parents were committed to the community in many ways, which meant that all their children were involved to varying degrees as well. For the most part, we all participated in different aspects of ministry in the church, from being a reader or minister of communion to singing in the choir or serving on the decorations committee. My parents also were committed financially and tithed from their income to their parish church. Along with their tithe came enrollment for any children in the parish school, which was for kindergarten through 8th grade. It worked out pretty well for my folks, I'm sure, since most of us got to go to private school and they didn't have to pay any more than they were already giving to the church.

I don't know if it is every Catholic mother's dream to have her son be a priest, but I do know that it was my mom's dream. With ten sons to choose from, the odds were really good. My uncle, her brother, was a priest in a small religious order called the Crosiers, and even though he died when I was in grade school, the idea of priesthood in our family was always on the table. I spent a lot of time around other religious communities as well because my father had two uncles who were priests and three aunts who were nuns – all from the same set of siblings. A spiritual destiny runs deep in my bloodline.

When I was in second grade, I, along with three girls who were my classmates, learned from one of the teachers at school how to play the guitar. We used our newfound skills for leading music at church. At first, it was just for our own grade level when we attended the weekly mass that was part of our routine. Soon, we were collaborating with some of the older kids at school, including one of my sisters, to lead the music when the entire student body was gathered. Before long, we were tapped to lead music at weekend services for the whole parish community.

When I was not leading music, I often served as an acolyte who assisted the priest directly at mass. Carrying things as we processed, ringing bells and preparing incense were among the duties I performed. In those days, it was only boys who were allowed to serve this way and I did not mind doing it at all. There were times when I got out of school to help with funerals, which involved a trip to the cemetery for a final blessing before the casket containing the body was lowered into the ground, including a special lunch put on by the church ladies and often a small stipend as a gift from the family – what young boy wouldn't want to do it, I thought?

I had been the object of quite a lot of belittling by some of the other boys in my school and I had a couple of friends from my class with whom I would hang out and play. Often our time together centered around homework and special academic projects, working together on the farm (theirs, my family lived in town) or doing something active like riding bikes or swimming. Besides the comfort of my few friends among the other boys, I would hang out with the girls which I found to be a whole lot easier and more pleasant than facing the ridicule of the class bullies.

After I finished 8th grade, I decided to attend a week-long camp called Summer Expo which was held at Crosier Seminary Prep, the high school run by the Crosiers (the order where my uncle had been a member) that was in a small town less than an hour away from where I grew up. I had such a good time, and learned all about the school and what it had to offer.

When I came home, I told my parents that I wanted to go there for high school, to which they wholeheartedly agreed.

For me, I had discovered a place where I could be among people who accepted me as a church music geek where that was really appreciated and celebrated. It was an escape for me also, from the bullying and ridicule I had experienced for hanging out with the girls and not being particularly athletic. For my parents, having seen me actively participate in church for many years at that point already, I think it was one more bright spot. By every measure, I was my mother's best hope to have a priest in the family and for me it was a very serious consideration.

I was the only kid in my freshman class of 36 at Crosier who played guitar and became involved with leading music every time we gathered for any form of worship or prayer together. I was elected class president that first year, and by being in leadership, felt a kinship with many of the priests and brothers whose school I was attending. By my second year, I was one of a handful of students tasked with planning all the worship services and music for the entire school. It felt like a natural fit for me, and I continued in that role for several more years involved in one way or another at Crosier.

The Catholicism I was fed as a child, under my parents' guidance, was one where sin and divine judgment were key features. It was in about 8th grade when I first began to question that theology and feel in my heart that something about it did not sit right with me. I began to explore the idea that divine love is far more powerful than judgment of any kind. When I went away to boarding school at Crosier, I found a more inclusive and welcoming environment where open questioning and spiritual exploration was tolerated to a certain degree.

I say to a degree because it was always within the context of a Catholic Church experience, and I discovered that breaking the paradigm I was raised with was not something that would happen overnight. I was deeply engrained in a Catholic culture and was even digging in deeper with my involvement and leadership within the system.

It was there, in high school, where I got to experience more of an insider's view of the Church. I spent a lot of time around priests and brothers who were decidedly human and rather crass about the Church itself. They taught me how to drink – a lot – and I saw some of them whose words and actions were miles apart. I learned of the secret lives some of them led, without the knowledge of the community to which they had professed their heart and soul.

Being involved in a community – both at school and with my family in my hometown – totally centered around a life in the Catholic Church, I didn't really know anything else. I simultaneously found myself embracing the familiar and questioning all of it.

In the last semester that I spent at Crosier, I was told by one of the priests with whom I had been sharing in spiritual direction counseling, that he thought they had done all they could for me and I ought to consider not coming back the next year. I remember thinking he was crazy. Here I was, an excellent student, never in trouble and the poster child for everything they might want as a future priest and he was telling me to go away. I was taken aback, but ultimately, after a lot of soul-searching over the summer, I decided to leave Crosier and attend my hometown public high school for my last year. I was with many of the same kids I had grown up with and still knew well because of our ongoing participation together in the youth group at our parish church and through doing many retreats together.

As I looked to college, I applied to several schools to study music, and ended up at the University of St. Thomas – you guessed it, Catholic! – in St. Paul. I was on autopilot, I think, when I went there, as the program I enrolled in was in Liturgical Music. I was following the next logical step from where I had been rather than focusing on where I truly wanted to go. Nonetheless, I dove in head first, and became not only a student in the program, but quickly got hired through my work-study to be the assistant to the director of the program.

The more involved I got, the more I realized what I thought I had been destined to do through music, was not going to be possible for me. The insider's view I got there was of professional church musicians, many of whom were there because they were well trained and felt like they needed the job. I met too many people to count who felt no connection to the spiritual community they were serving and I became very disillusioned.

The impact of seeing clergy who were not committed to what they had professed pretty well sealed the deal that I would not be pursuing priesthood for myself. I felt like the whole idea of it was a sham. I knew in my core that doing something half-heartedly was not for me and I saw the giant chasm between what were the official teachings of the Church and what got put into practice by its leaders on the ground, the clergy. It became clear to me that I did not want to be part of perpetuating a dichotomy like this but that did not stop my desire to be of service to people spiritually.

I was so deeply programmed as a Catholic that it was hard for me to see anything else as an option at that time. I continued on for several more years of being within a system with which I was not in harmony. I tried to ignore the parts of the system I did not like and surround myself with people who felt the same way I did – love was the answer, not fear and judgment. This worked for a while until I found myself up against the words that the whole community recited together every week and myself sitting there in silence. I felt totally disconnected from the language we were using and began translating almost every word I uttered during services.

Throughout my years in college, I had these ideas of an idealized community and of changing things from within, but my passion for transformation was growing further and further from the behemoth of organized religion.

I was deep in the mud of church music, and consequently, the Church itself. I saw how jaded some of the long-time professionals were and I felt that my heart could not stand that for me. It appeared to me they were living a double life and I did not want to end up the same way. Even though I had no idea what I would do, I felt strongly that a career in liturgical music was definitely not for me and I abandoned the program when I had less than a year to complete it.

While leaving gave me some relief from the internal struggles I had faced around my career options, it left me feeling rudderless. I had been defined by my Catholic-ness and being a church musician my entire life and now I was facing a life without all of that, which felt lonely and I was really scared.

In my post-Catholic recovery period, at first I felt like I had something to recover from. Initially, I felt like I had been duped and I had a reason to be angry about it. It took me a while, but eventually I realized that my upbringing had made me the person I was and that it was all good. The only way I could change the past was to think differently about it and that gave me a new perspective, a way to embrace all of who I had been and who

I was becoming. I also found a creative outlet that served me very well and took up architectural design as a means of earning a living and feeding my mind, body and even my soul.

Over a few years, I tried a variety of spiritual teachings and practices, which ranged from other Christian denominations to meditation, yoga and pagan rituals celebrating the seasons. I discovered that none of them was a panacea with all the answers. There were none of them that resonated with me in full, but rather, I have gleaned great value in bits and pieces from many to use off and on throughout my life. Some have found their way into my regular and daily practice like a one-breath centering where I have learned I can reset in pretty much any situation.

I have always enjoyed reading books, magazines and other literary formats. I had gotten used to reading inspirational poetry and the bible while in high school at Crosier mostly through being on retreats, and sharing that experience with friends. In 1992, I was introduced to the book, *Way of the Peaceful Warrior* and it totally rocked my world. The subtitle, *A Book That Changes Lives* was particularly apt for me because it opened my eyes to a whole new realm of possibility where my life was mine to live on purpose.

That one book began a journey from book-to-book and teacher-to-teacher. It was a total shift from where I had been. I found myself exploring spiritual teachings from ancient poetry to modern fiction and the latest scientific breakthroughs, curious about what would be coming next for humanity and the planet. For people who absorb the news, the future might seem bleak, like we are headed downhill so fast there is no way to stop or even slow down fast enough to make any difference. On the flip side, all the studying I have done has left me feeling totally optimistic and hopeful. I discovered the commonality in all of what I was taking in was that the idea of universal Oneness was front and center. I felt at home with that idea and its offspring of love over fear.

My spiritual exploration has been an outstanding companion. It has challenged me to see myself in a different light and helped me to help other people discover their own path. I was asked to officiate at the wedding of one of my brothers so, using the internet method, I got ordained so their marriage would be official and legal. Having that status has allowed me to help many other couples get married as well, which has been very rewarding and great fun to be of service.

Along the way, though, I resisted becoming a spiritual leader out of fear I couldn't measure up to the vision my mother had of her priest-son. I had been playing a very small game, all the while knowing in my heart my talents were not being put to their best use. I felt there had to be a greater purpose to my existence, that I had somehow missed my calling. I found myself searching for more. More of what, I did not know. More of me, I guess. It was a deep longing that did not seem to go away, one that I felt in my heart and one I felt a little guilty about having because so many things seemed to be going well for me.

I could see visions of a great future and ideas swirling around in my head for what could contribute to that greatness, yet I was missing from my own script. In every version of the vision, there were plenty of friends, family and organizations creating that amazing future and I saw myself as being a supporting character, always with someone else who would be in the spotlight. I heard voices in my head talking to me saying that nobody would listen to me anyway so I might as well just sit down and shut up. "Go back to what you know – you've got that down. Don't rock the boat."

Through the ongoing teacher-to-teacher flow I had been enjoying for many years, I ended up being introduced to the message of Oneness as delivered by Bob Proctor and Sandy Gallagher. What I discovered inside was my self-image was the culprit for where I saw myself in those future visions and for where I was presently too. I saw myself as limited and unworthy of the life I had imagined and that is why I showed up in a supporting role rather than have the lead in the movie of my own life.

I could now see myself leading a team of people, working harmoniously together. As somewhat of a global futurist and a decided optimist with a desire to make a big impact on people and the planet, I found out that I had been holding myself back from something much bigger. The voice in my head started in again, "Who do you think you are, Jay? Sit your skinny butt down and keep quiet already!" I even heard my mother's voice asking, "What will people think?"

It was at this point I started to put two and two together and could see how my skills and life-well-lived transforming spaces through architectural design had been equally about transforming the lives of the people who lived in those spaces. I had too many clients to name who reminded me every time I saw them how they loved the space we created for them to use every day, how their lives were much better because I solved a previously insurmountable design challenge. There were even a few couples who told me that because of the way we redesigned their space it had saved their marriage. Who knew you could do that with a drafting pencil, right? I had been engaged in transformationalism as an architectural design practice, and with people's lives though I didn't know it at the time.

In 2015, I took part in a week-long event put on by Proctor Gallagher Institute called Matrixx. When I began to meet and interact with the other participants, I felt totally at home. There were people from all over the world, every age and station in life, each there with different levels of big ideas to discover and execute, and each also there to fully participate and contribute to the whole group. It became increasingly clear to me that I was on the right track and landed exactly where I needed to be.

How could I be so sure? My desire to serve people is a seed that was planted way back when I learned to play the guitar in second grade. I discovered that desire had only been partially realized. When I was a kid leading music at church and school, it was a way to bring people together with one voice. When I was a teenager, besides music, I became involved in student government and one of only a few teens who were consistently involved in leading retreats for other teens and adults alike. Throughout my adult life, I have been called upon by friends and family as a sort of spiritual guide too many times to count. At Matrixx, I found myself being challenged to step it up a (very big) notch and had other participants working through all sorts of different questions with me one-on-one and in small groups. I didn't purposely say I was there for that, but it was happening automatically, and naturally.

When I was first introduced to the writings of Neale Donald Walsch (in 1998), it spurred me to begin writing a book where science and spirituality intersect. At the time, I wrote only a few pages before I shut myself down with my internal stories of how I wasn't good enough and why it didn't matter anyway.

Seventeen years later, the ember of becoming an author I had set aside got fanned in a way I can only describe as miraculous. Less than three months after meeting a mentor to work with, Peggy McColl, I had finished my initial draft of *Architect of Being: Easily Create Your Dream Life from the Foundation Up*. She and my editor both helped to keep me constantly focused on my readers and what would be of maximum benefit for them. Even as I was writing the book, I was also thinking far beyond it to offering other transformational services to help people achieve their goals, connect with others and transform themselves and the world. It took a couple more months to have a final-final version we all felt was worthy of my name and would be worth the investment of time and money for readers.

With Peggy's guidance and the help of her sister, Judy, a self-publishing expert, I pursued promoting the book on Amazon.com. It became a #1 bestseller in two countries and hit top-ten status in fourteen categories. I had set a goal to become a bestselling author and the day I achieved it was one of the most emotional moments of my life. I was literally overcome with tears of joy and gratitude for everybody who had contributed to the success of Architect of Being. I felt myself expanding in ways far beyond what I had ever imagined and yet, because of the clarity of my goal, it was as if I had already experienced it and the actual achievement was just a formality.

I found my voice for transformation by listening to my heart rather than the voices in my head telling me I was not fit for service. I finally realized I could trust my Self, to trust the connection I feel to other people and all of life. I discovered life happens by action. Whether that action is conscious or unconscious does not matter in the least, it is still the action of my life. It is in listening to my heart, tuning into the flow of 'All That Is' and getting up and doing something – anything – to move in the direction of the big visions I have that they will continue to be realized.

Having left the comfort of the familiar, I am operating outside the structure of a large organization where the rules would be clear. That means the only rules are the ones I place on myself. Now, that is something both liberating and terrifying. Having the freedom of self-determination is an awesome power and with that also comes the awesome responsibility to serve the greatest good I know at any given moment. I'm sure I'll stumble and step on some toes without knowing any better but that will also be how I learn to walk in bigger, far gentler shoes.

Anyone is welcome on this journey – the journey of discovering yourself, your natural, transformationalist power and your own **destiny**. My path began deeply rooted in the ideals of Catholicism and the dreams of my mother that were even more deeply rooted. By trusting my intuition and acting on it I have grown to know in my heart I am on the right path. I know that my expression of All That Is is in perfect harmony with my destiny to live life on purpose for the benefit of the most people I can possibly reach. With every step I take, a little more light shines out and a little less fear tries to stop me.

Let your light shine bright – the world needs you!

ABOUT JAY

Jay Billig is the founder of New Thought Forum, author of the international bestselling book, *Architect of Being* as well as a teacher, mentor and coach who has been inspiring people to dream big and creatively transform their own lives for over 20 years. After attending The University of St. Thomas in St. Paul, without graduating, he decided to follow his desire for service and move to Austin, Texas, where he learned from seasoned leaders – and taught himself – what he needed to be a successful entrepreneur in residential building, architectural design and real estate investment. He spent over two decades helping people transform their lives by transforming their spaces. Jay's unique gift is that he seamlessly blends science, spirituality and practical tools to help individuals and organizations transform the space within themselves so that their presence in the world is transformed. Born in Little Falls, MN into an eclectic clan of thirteen siblings, Jay's personal path of transformation is ongoing and his love of discovering new ideas is a constant companion. Jay, his partner, and their five children, are citizens of the earth, with a particular fondness for Austin, Texas.

HOW THE WATER CHANGED MY LIFE

BY REGINE C. HENSCHEL

Something was wrong. I had an amazing job writing books and articles. I worked in a famous architectural office, I had a wooden desk, I enjoyed a great view over the river, and I met interesting designers and architects every day. My friends thought I lived a happy life, but I thought something was missing. Every weekend I went to the North Sea, and I collected shells, sat at the Mole and drank hot coffee. Regardless of the season, I sat at the beach and thought about life.

I worked as a writer for newspapers, television, and architectural design books. I had studied philosophy, but I was worried about working in my field. I had been told that philosophy jobs didn't pay well and, as a result, philosophers often had to resort to working as taxi drivers.

One day, I was sitting at the Mole, watching birds fly over the sea, and I thought to myself: "Wouldn't it be wonderful to write about the water? Wouldn't it be great to write about the things I love? I wonder, who would be interested in reading about the things I love?" These questions remained on my mind the entire day. I had no idea how to make the transition to writing about topics I enjoyed.

The next day, someone from my office told me about an interesting project. They had built a house near the harbor, and they needed someone to document it and take pictures of the house with a photographer.

I screamed, "Yes, that's a project for me!" It was a beautiful and cozy house. I enjoyed interviewing the architects and designers. I had the opportunity to talk to them about their ideas for the house, but I soon realized that it was not the house itself which attracted me. Instead, it was the experience of being near the water, the beauty of the harbor, the smell of the sea, the crashing waves, and the special magic of feeling free. I was reminded of my interest in writing about the magnetic force of water.

One day, I was on a train travelling to a big architectural fair in Germany. The train was overcrowded and I was seated in the restaurant wagon. I ordered a glass of my favorite wine, sat near the window, took out my book, and read *You were Born Rich* by Bob Proctor. I read the chapter about 'Vibrations and Attitude'. As people got off the train and new ones came on, I sat and read. Suddenly, someone sat at my table and ordered a tea. I did not acknowledge him. I simply did not want to be disturbed. I continued to read my book, nonetheless I could feel the person staring at me. I tried to ignore him, but I was unable to concentrate.

"Who on earth is that?" I thought to myself. I shut my book and looked up at the man. He smiled at me and then looked at his teapot. He looked like he was in his late 40's. He was dressed in blue, British-styled clothing and seemed old fashioned. As the train crossed a bridge, over a valley and a small river, I heard myself saying "Isn't that beautiful?" "Yes," said the man to my surprise. This sparked a conversation about nature and the water.

During the course of the conversation, I learned that he was Dr. Bernd Kröplin, a professor of aerospace science, and a famous water researcher in Europe. They called him the "Water Pope". I could not believe that I had met him in an overcrowded train. We had a deep discussion about the water, its ability to store information, and the memory of water. Suddenly, he opened his huge black travelling bag and showed me some slides, which he had prepared for a lecture at a conference. He gave me the slides without saying a word.

"These are water drops," I exclaimed. "Yes, these are drops of different types of water, dried under our darkfield microscope in the lab." It was amazing; every water type had its own structure. Water was distinguishable from Black Sea water. Tap water was distinguishable from a water desalination machine. Water isn't just water! Water has many faces. "Water is like a mirror," explained the professor. "It reflects where it came from, and it reflects the impact of its environment." I was excited and I wanted to learn more.

Professor Kröplin told me his research team was holding an exhibition about the memory and secrets of water at the renowned European World Exhibition Expo 2000 in Hannover. I knew I wanted to attend the exhibition as soon as possible. He gave me his business card and said, "After you attend the exhibition, I would like to speak to you about your thoughts on our research." Then he stood up, picked up his heavy black bag with hundreds of water drop slides, and got off the train at the next station. I just sat there. I was astonished. I realized something special just happened to me. I gazed out the window and thought about how I would respond to this experience.

The following weekend, I attended the exhibition. Professor Kröplin and his team showed dried water droplets from around the world. I recognized some of the water droplets from the slides he had shown me on the train. I realized the pictures of water drops told a story – of where they came from, and what they have seen in their 'water drop life'. Their story told me if they were impacted by mobile phone or x-ray radiation, if they 'listened' to music, or if they had experienced a negative emotion. It was amazing! Water reacts like a human being to things that happens in its environment as reflected in the structure of the water drop if it was exposed to classical music, pop, or hard rock. Water droplets store everything that vibrates, even the information of plants and stones.

I read that Professor Kröplin and his team initially studied how weak fields impact astronauts in space. They studied low impacts of radiation that have never been measured before, as there is no device for measuring them. The impact was apparent by the change in structures of the water droplets in their pictures. We can see low vibrations with the naked eye! Things that were previously invisible to us are visible in water drops. "What a great phenomenon!" I thought.

I spend the day at the exhibition, and I didn't leave until it closed. I wanted to learn about how all these amazing things happen because our body is composed of up to 70% water, including cell water, urine, lymph, and blood. We are water beings. Therefore, it is very important to understand how water functions in our bodies. I wondered if Professor Kröplin could answer my questions about water. Did he know why my blood reflects my favorite music or my emotions? How would this impact me, my environment, my body, and my life?

I phoned him the following Monday morning. He was in his car driving to the institute where he worked. I was hoping he would remember me – the woman on the train who was blown away by his research. I didn't know how he would react if I told him I wanted to learn more about water. I told him what I thought about his ideas and the exhibition. I was sure I said too much, too loudly, and too enthusiastically. He didn't say anything when I stopped talking, but I knew he was still on the phone because I heard the noise of his car.

"Mmmhmm," he said very calmly. "That´s alright, it's interesting how you explain that." I did not remember the rest of our conversation except for the end of it. Professor Kröplin said, "We are looking for someone who may support us in our water research and public relations." "Did I tell you I am a journalist?" I yelled so that he could hear me over the noise of his car. "Yes, you did," he answered. I was sure he was smiling. I was excited for the opportunity. Professor Kröplin told me he would expect my application for the job.

I could not believe it. I knew I had to submit my application for such an amazing job. I would get the opportunity to work with water, my passion. This research was too good to be ignored, and I wanted to spread the word about water. Although I was excited, I knew this opportunity would change my life. I lived in the north of Germany, and the institute was in the south. I would have to move all my furniture and personal belongings. I would have to quit my job at the architectural office near the river and the sea. In the end, I decided to leave my job in hopes of something better. I needed to understand my attraction to water.

I quit my job and, unfortunately, many obstacles followed. My chief did not want to let me go and said, "We need you here." My friends were not amused either. "What do you want in the south of Germany? It's completely different! In the south, there are mountains, but here, you have the sea!" As if this was not enough, I could not find my certificate which verified I had studied philosophy and literature. I was required to send a copy of my certificate with my job application to Professor Kröplin. Up until now, I didn't need my certificate because no one ever asked, they only ever wanted to know if I could write articles – and I could. After my unsuccessful search, I asked the secretary of my old university to send me a verified copy of my graduate certificate. She sent it to me within a week. What wonderful luck!

I sent my application to the Professor Kröplin, however, I did not receive a response. Time went by and I was in the final days of my work at the architectural office. I had planned my move, and already ordered a moving van. I had terminated the lease for my flat on the island, and finished my articles for the architectural office. Still, I had not received a message from the water professor. I went to the sea, sat at the Mole, drank my last coffee at the wonderful harbor, and watched the birds. I thought to myself, "What should I do?" I had not yet been offered the job, tomorrow was my last day at my old job, the moving van was scheduled to come on Saturday, and I had already rented a small flat in the south.

I saw a little bird sitting at the end of a roof top. It was a seagull with white and grey shining feathers. "It will fly away in a few seconds," I thought to myself. Suddenly, it fell off the roof edge, but milliseconds later, it spread its wings and flew! "That's it. You have to fall – and then you have to fly. Thank you, little bird! I will do just that!" I said to myself.

The next day was my last day at the office. My colleagues stood around my desk, celebrating my farewell by drinking champagne and eating cake. "Did you hear back about the job?" my friend Max asked. "Not yet," I answered. "What? You don't know if you got the job and you quit your job, your flat and all relationships!" exclaimed another colleague. Max was embarrassed because he didn't want me to get in trouble by discussing this with my old colleagues. "Well," I said, "I don't have it now, but I will get it at the right time." I spoke with confidence. "Hopefully," responded my colleagues. It was clear they couldn´t understand what I was doing.

After my discussion with my colleagues, my short farewell party was over. I washed the glasses, boxed the leftover cake, and collected the bottles. Suddenly, I heard a bing. I had new mail in my inbox. I walked over to the computer and opened the mail. It was from the water professor. He only wrote two sentences: "The University is okay with your appointment. Isn't that good?" "Yes, it was," I thought, and took a deep, deep breath. "Just in time!"

To make a long story short, Professor Kröplin is now my colleague and, between you and me, he still does not talk much, just like many scientists. I moved to the Institute for Statics and Dynamics of Aerospace Structures and, after one and a half years, we founded TAO Group in Stuttgart, this means trans atmospheric operations – all inventions between earth and space. Together with Dr. Bernd Kröplin, I run the company. Our team invents new technologies for the future that are beneficial for humankind, such as new water desalination machines, sun storages powered by water mist, and water batteries. I remain most interested in the research about the memory of water.

My first meeting with Professor Kröplin led to an amazing story. When I research water in my lab, I often experience goose bumps because it has such a phenomenal relevance in our lives. Our bodies communicate with water at different levels, such as: on a physical level; when we look at a river; look at the sea, as I did when I was sitting at the Mole; when we bathe; when we drink; or when we wash.

We communicate on a deep, subconscious level with water. Sometimes, we can sense when we feel attracted to water, or when we think about the fact that water has always played an important role in all cultures in mythology or astrophysics. "The reflecting surface, moving or still, the quiet, mysterious depth, the flowing, rippling, dripping, rustling, smelling, tasting, feeling of the water on the skin or the feeling of being carried by the water are primal experiences. Water in the mythologies means mind. It has inspired man in his creative power", explains Prof. Dr. Bernd Kröplin in his book *The World in a Drop – Memory and Forms of Thought in Water*.

Water contains, in effect and application, numerous mysteries, which are not yet fully explored. For us, in our 'world in a drop' water research, I think the mystery of the 'memory' of water is particularly interesting. Let's do a theoretical experiment like we do every day in our lab.

Imagine what would happen if:

- Water has a memory? Would the sea know of the spring, and would the spring, perhaps, know of the sea?
- Water talks? Would there be a transfer of information in the water?
- Water is a mirror in which we could recognize the world?

"Our view in the world traditionally divides between natural and human sciences, between the world of the measurable and the world of unprovable concepts. But reality is what works and not everything that works is measurable. Otherwise, the first great love would not have been a reality and the trust of your children only appearance. Otherwise, there would be no honor or ethics. As we now see in the water drops, they are talking to each other, while information and mental energy seem to produce systematic changes. It is worthwhile to at least look at them. Because this could be the measurable beginning of what we all intuitively know, namely, that the mind permeates matter and that thoughts manifest themselves much more extensively in material structuring than we think," explains Prof. Kröplin.

To thoroughly understand this quote, I learned to write authentically about the phenomena, using the darkfield microscope. My first experiments were with flowers and water. I put flowers in water, took some drops, and photographed them under a darkfield microscope. It was amazing, the information from the flowers changed the water droplet picture. The next day, I put crystals and gems in fresh water because materials and substances from rock crystals cannot dissolve in water. The water picture changed again, but in a different way. Every plant and every crystal created its own water droplet picture.

One month later, more challenging experiments were performed to research water's communication. Over 50,000 photos have been classified over the last 15 years. We have studied water from all over the world. Once, we studied water from a former daytime mine near Berlin. It was interesting to see a radiant spiky edge on the image of the drop, as if it was separated by a barbed wire fence. That's why we called it "Berlin Water".

We have since tried to break the 'fence' by dripping other water close to the Berlin Water drop on a glass slide. We chose Ganges water. It is considered to be sacred, and we thought that it might 'break' the water of Berlin. Although we placed drops of the Ganges water right next to the water of Berlin, nothing happened. We continued testing with other types of water. When we placed a drop of water from a pure mountain spring beside the Berlin Water drop, the spiky fence ring opened, both drops merged into each other, and exchanged information. They 'communicated', which is why we named it water communication.

Water communication seems to work like someone who has a green thumb. Some people connect with flowers and plants, and some don't. It depends on their energy. Everybody has energy, and the body sends this energy to the environment. This energy connects with plants, water, and the environment. You can witness this by using a special camera developed in 1937 by Kirlian. We can witness the different energy of people when we perform experiments where each person places a drop of the same type of water on a slide. The resulting water droplet structure is different for each person. This illustrates the strong influence of the experimenter on the water.

One day, I saw the power of love. I saw the power of good and healthy emotions. I sat in my lab and I was thinking about someone with whom I am deeply in love. I thought about this person and placed water drops onto the glass slide. When I looked at the drops under the darkfield microscope as they were drying, a shape of a heart appeared in the structure of the water drop. The heart contained sparkling stars and a dot in the centre surrounded by a light blue color. I photographed it and thought, "This should be on the cover of a water book about our research." One year later, my dream came true and we published our photo book *The Seven Secrets of Water – Communication and Thoughts in Water.*

"It would be wonderful if more people around the world read about our amazing secrets of water," I thought. We had exhibitions in Austria, India, and Mexico, however, we didn't publish our photo book internationally. Once again, my wish resonated with something and someone in the world. I participated in the Goal Achiever Seminar and heard Bob Proctor talking about a new book project called *Destiny* with Peggy McColl. I thought to myself, "That's it! I would love to share our story in their book." I am excited I got the opportunity to tell our story in this wonderful book.

How do our thoughts materialize? I think about how it happened to me. In terms of water research, we are just at the beginning. We still have so much more to study. We have empirical evidence that drops of water 'talk' to one another. When information and mental energy seem to generate systematic changes, it is worthwhile to investigate it further. It could be the measurable beginning of what we all know intuitively, that mind permeates matter and that thoughts manifest themselves in material structures much more extensively than we now think possible.

As an individual, you are reflected in water, like in a mirror. When the water moves, you can see your real and distorted reflection. If you have a strong emotion, like shock, you can see it in the structure of your saliva or water. Also, our favorite music leaves traces in the water drop, that is, in the cell water. Your blood, for example, clearly changes its structure under the darkfield microscope if you have heard relaxing music, such as classical music from Satie, or your most beloved meditation music.

We think that everything that you positively resonate with, any positive information, affirmation or good idea, as well as love and sympathy, changes your own body water, and that of others. If your body water resonates positively with someone, sympathy may be the result, because the two bodies may exchange their information by resonating water. This happens subconsciously. Our body water even reacts to vibrations from voices and music heard on phone calls or over the radio. If you listen to a beautiful voice that resonates with you, such as on the radio or the voice of your loved one on the phone, it also affects your body water.

Quantum physics postulates that spirit moves matter. This idea is applicable to our daily lives. We see it in water, an odorless, colorless, formless, tasteless element, and the subject of my research. Is it quantum physics that attracted me to research water, or is it due to the properties of water? We are facing a substantial upheaval that could guide us into a new era of humanity. We have discovered a new understanding of matter that assigns humans to the role of co-creator, or, more specifically, the intellectual designer of the world.

Considering the current research on the secrets of water, it has become very important to me to be aware of: what I think every day; my environment; and the kind of people with whom I surround myself. Everything is relevant and it has an impact on my body water, my cells, and my life. People should be aware of the powerful possibilities. Document this in our water research, write about it, and explain it to people – that is my **destiny**.

Quotes were taken from lectures, The Seven Secrets of Water – Communication and Thoughts in Water *by Prof. Dr. Bernd-Helmut Kröplin and Regine C. Henschel, and from the exhibition under the same name. Further information and publications can be found at www.worldinadrop.com*

ABOUT REGINE

Regine C. Henschel (M.A.) wants to know what the world is all about. After obtaining her Masters of Arts Degree in Philosophy and Literary Studies, she worked as a TV editor for German television stations such as Arte, ZDF and 3Sat focusing on science and culture. She worked as a press and public relations consultant for various corporate companies in the fields of design, architecture, and construction. Ms. Henschel has also worked at "World in a Drop". She worked with Prof. Dr. Bernd Kröplin at the Institute for Statics and Dynamics of Aerospace Structures at the University of Stuttgart and since 2001 at TAO Group. She is an author of several books including *The Seven Secrets of Water – Communication and Thoughts in Water*. In 2001, she co-founded TAO Group with Prof. Bernd Kröplin. TAO Group is an international research and development company for human and water-friendly technologies of the future.

For more information on their groundbreaking research, please visit www.tao-group.de and www.worldinadrop.com.

WELCOMING ADVERSITY AS MY DESTINY

By George Chung

What if I told you to search for adversity?

What if I shared with you that building a business around adversity motivates and inspires success?

What if I thought that adversity is the greatest magnet for growth?

It might sound crazy that I actually strive for adversity, but I am confident after learning more about my journey, you'll be excited about making adversity part of your own.

I have always enjoyed the success of being a dominant real estate agent. From the day I began my business, a contrarian approach to the industry helped me reach a level I couldn't have ever imagined.

My journey to that end started while attending Seoul Foreign School in Seoul, Korea. While there, and in the eighth grade, the school awarded a Math Cup to the best overall math student. The school originally created the award in memory of a student who excelled in math, but tragically passed away very early in his life. Before the school year even started, I decided I would win it. To get a head start on the competition, I began in earnest to dig into my lessons. As the year progressed, it became clear to me I had only one other student who stood a real chance against me. In the end, only a few points separated the winner from the runner up. I took the victory, and realized some important lessons in the process. First, I set a goal early in the school year, knowing it would create adversity for me.

I would have to study more, sacrifice television and fun with friends, and be willing to outwork the other students… and I did. I knew there was no place on the cup for the name of the runner up. Winning the cup was even a bigger deal, since I was the first Korean student to take first. This was just the beginning of setting adversarial goals and working towards them.

I attended UCLA after high school, entered the School of Engineering, and taught myself a very important lesson that strengthened my resolve in any undertaking. At the time, I was reflecting on how hard it was for my parents to support me through college. My room and board cost a little over one hundred dollars. That might seem like a small amount of money today, but that was a king's ransom in my hometown in Korea. I made a decision I would support myself by working part time, and subsidizing this with student loans. I wrote a letter to my parents and told them to stop sending me money, which they did. I created this adversity to up my game. I had to scramble and find odd jobs at first just to make ends meet. As I expanded my search at the university placement center, I noticed an ad for a math tutor. Although I had not tutored before, math was one of my favorite subjects. I began tutoring primary and junior high school students in math. It was quite rewarding to help students improve their grades, and many of my mentees increased their scores by an entire grade. During this time, I learned you cannot really understand a subject unless you can teach it to someone else. As I became more proficient at tutoring, I raised my fee to $10 per hour. I could comfortably pay my room and board and still have funds left over for some fun and an occasional 'steak and stein'. Once again, I declined the safe and easy way out – my parents support. Rather, I did it on my own. That adversity helped me become an expert in math and numbers, skills I'd use for the rest of my life.

During the summer between my sophomore and junior years, I had a roommate named Scott. He was an extra in showbiz. One day, he awoke at 5:00AM to work on a movie set. He returned at 8:00AM that same day; I was curious why he returned so quickly, and asked if he had been fired? He laughed, and indicated he had done a 'silent bit'. He shared with me what a silent bit was.. My ears perked up when Scott told me he was paid $70.00 for just a couple hours of work. I wanted to do the same. Scott told me I should register with the various casting offices and secure at least one job. After that, I could join the Screen Extras Guild (SEG) and work towards more regular parts. I did, and began regularly working in film.

This offered an extremely flexible opportunity for me. I could pick and choose the days I wanted to work by calling the various casting offices the day before. Of course, there were days I was unable to secure work, but those were in the minority. As I got knee deep into acting, I found it rather strange the extras were not eager to work on the set, and would play cards or read a book, even though they were being paid handsomely to be in the background. I could have easily done the same, however, an extra could make more income on set if they participated in the storyline. The movie industry called this a 'bump'. More close-up work equal more pay. Why not? As the importance of the extra in the scene grew, that extra might receive two or three bumps. Eventually, an extra could secure a silent bit, where that person he or she became part of the story line but had no spoken words. Since showbiz was a new industry for me, I wanted to learn as much as possible and stay in the game.

I learned that each day of shooting consisted of a script breakdown, which included the scenes to be shot for the day. If you wanted to find out what the production company was shooting that day, all you had to do was get a hold of the script breakdown. Whenever I went to work on a movie set, this was the first thing I did. I would make friends with the electrician, gaffer, lighting assistant, sound assistant, or camera assistant, and then ask if I could borrow their script breakdown. I quickly read the script and looked at the breakdown for the day, determining which scenes were most important. I became pretty good at determining which scenes could offer multiple bumps. I would then stay in the deep background, meaning where there was no way you could recognize me on film. When the scene with the 'money' came up and the director asked the assistant director who wasn't seen in the foreground, my name would naturally come up. They'd often choose me to be in the scene with the principal actor which came with the extra pay.

I excelled at this, and my colleagues nicknamed me 'Silent Bit Chung'. There were two television shows I consistently worked on under my stage name 'Byron Chung'. The first was *Room 222*, and the other was *M*A*S*H*. As an undergraduate student at UCLA, *Room 222* was the ideal television show for me. I was one of the students in the classroom, so I could show up in my normal wardrobe of jeans and a T-shirt. On top of that, they shot their outdoor scenes at Dorsey High School, about seven miles east of UCLA. Whenever a movie company shot on location, they had to give a per diem for mileage and even feed you on the set. I was in student heaven.

The movie company paid me, fed me, allowed me to study, and gave me transportation money. As I continued acting, my show biz break came while working on *Room 222*. During my time on set, I became friends with the second assistant director, first assistant director, and eventually with producer/director Gene Reynolds. Andy, the second assistant, knew I was a hard worker. One day, there was an actor part in the script. Gene asked the second assistant for someone to do the part. It was literally one word but in those days, if you spoke even one word, you would have to be a member of the Screen Actors Guild (SAG). The production company sent me to the casting office to sign the SAG contracts. While I was waiting to sign the contract, there was a theatrical agent who asked if I had an agent? I did not. She invited me to her office for an interview. I accepted. When I got to her office, she had contracts ready for me to sign. Before I knew it, I had a theatrical (movies and television) agent.

In the beginning, I lost count as to how many auditions she sent me to and didn't get. I met an actress who befriended me, and advised that I quit trying to act. She told me to 'become' the character, and then 'read' the lines from the perspective of that character. It worked like a charm, and I began picking up acting gigs. One of them was on *M*A*S*H*, in which I played various Korean parts.

During the second quarter of my last year while in the UCLA's MBA curriculum, I landed a part on a pilot called *PROBE*, starring Hugh O'Brian and Burgess Meredith. The show was sold as a series called *Search*, and I was offered to be a series regular the month before I completed my MBA. At that time, there were very limited opportunities in the job market for an engineer graduate with an MBA degree. I had to decide whether to accept what I considered a low paying corporate job, or hang around to see how my acting career would unfold. Since I was young and full of adventure, I decided to accept the semi-regular role of 'Kuroda' in the series.

While on set, I discovered I had an excess amount of time in between my shooting days. I wanted to find something to fill in the gap. At the time, I already had a real estate license, and decided to work for a real estate company on a part time basis. I would double my workload, but could also double my earning potential.

When I started working for the real estate company, I went around the office to find the most successful salesmen and women. I learned the agents who made the most telephone solicitation calls were the most successful. I followed suit, and started to make cold calls. It was rough going at first, especially since I had no experience and no practical real estate training. Nevertheless, I was persistent and worked my way up to making over 800 cold calls per day. That may be hard to imagine, and there were only a half dozen agents making the same number of calls. Within 18 months, I was earning more income than the people I knew who were working as engineers for over ten years. I knew real estate was for me.

After a successful run as a salesperson, I decided to start my own real estate company with another salesperson from the same company. Because we were both good cold callers, we were an immediate success in the Westside of Los Angeles. We also started a mortgage company with a loan processor we had used before. This was the second time I started in real estate with no leads and direction but that didn't stop us from eventually building a large listing inventory. However, things hit a bump in the road when my partner betrayed me. There I was, broke and married with a pregnant wife, ready to begin again.

To that end, I decided to work with a large real estate company. I started in the training center. Since I was a well-trained cold caller, I put those skills to use and built a book of over 20 listings in only three months. Eventually, I wanted something different and I went to work for one of the three largest real estate companies in the Westside of Los Angeles, as an assistant to Fred Sands, one of the most successful real estate brokers of the modern era. As I became immersed into their corporate culture from the ninth floor corner office next to Fred, I learned a large real estate company is like a lumbering giant with more problems than you can imagine. After this brief employment, I joined Electronic Realty Associates, a National Franchise real estate company. Starting again and again was extremely adversarial, but it taught me I could build anything from scratch. It didn't matter where I was or for whom I worked. I could do it, and I had a proven track record of success.

Electronic Realty taught me the importance of dominating your listing market. Forget about being everything to everyone and everywhere. Pick a small radius and 'kill' it. Right as I switched, the real estate market entered the worst recession since the Great Depression era. Mortgage interest rates climbed to 16%, and people could not afford homes. It seemed like the real estate sales had declined by over 50% in that time. It was during this adverse time I had to make some major decisions. I knew I did not want to leave the real estate profession that provided me with such a happy lifestyle so I had to adapt. I did so by making three very important business decisions:

1. Adversity drives decisions.
2. Become a big frog in a small pond.
3. Utilize the one-mile radius rule.

First, I decided I would let adversity drive the train. Creating a business structure that made me uncomfortable would position me for success. It made me work harder and smarter.

Second, I would become a big frog in a small pond. I had to become the recognized expert, not just a general real estate agent.

Finally, to become a big frog, I would only represent sellers within a one-mile radius of my office.

Most agents would tell you this was a recipe for disaster. In a time when most agents were spreading out for more opportunity, I was anchoring my boat to only one dock. My office was on the corner of Beethoven Street and Palms Boulevard, in the Mar Vista area. That was my dock, and I would only travel within one mile of that office for listings. I realized that decision would help me save remarkable amounts of time and money. I wouldn't have long drives in Los Angeles traffic, or weak relationships with distant brokers. If I accomplished this, I would know everyone, and be widely recognized as the guy for this small market. I toured more houses that were all within my self-defined target market area. My knowledge of this market quickly accelerated. Now I just had to solve the issue of rising mortgage rates. This didn't prove to be so easy, but I reverted to my eighth-grade Math Cup championship trophy. While all the other agents were waiting for mortgage rates to 'return to earth', I did something about it.

After looking at the problem from as many angles as possible, and with a little bit of creative imagination, I came up with a solution. I asked: What if I could reduce the mortgage rates for a new homebuyer to 12% the first year, and then let it float upwards at 1% per year until it reached the peak of 16%? In other words, what if the interest on their mortgage payments for the first year was 12%, then 13% the second year, 14% the third year,

15% the fourth year, and 16% the fifth year. When I interviewed potential buyers, they initially rejected this proposal so I had to take the additional step of finding out the profession of the buyers, and how their income might change. After plugging the numbers, I could show most buyers that, while their mortgage payments might increase by 7.5% per month each year, their income was increasing on average by 10%, which would offset the increase in their mortgage. As I continued the conversations with my buyers, it became abundantly clear to them that this could work.

Napoleon Hill said, "Adversity carries a seed of an equivalent or greater benefit." I learned that throughout my life, and I wanted to apply this standard to my clients. Sure, they were introducing adversity into their lives, but it would push them to remain employed, work hard, and try to advance in their own careers to withstand their additional financial obligations. Through listening to my clients, assessing their needs, and coming to a thoughtful and cognizant resolution for them, I was able to buck the trends and start selling more houses than anyone else in my market. Continuing down this path, I eventually captured over 50% of the market share within one mile of my office. We had the largest listing market share than all the real estate companies combined including all the large real estate companies with dozens of offices and thousands of agents in the area.

My agency is now a big frog in a small pond, and we operate at an extraordinarily lean and harmonious level. In life, you will face adversity. Interest rates will be high, but you always have to adjust. Even today, I refuse to serve buyers outside of my little pond. Some agents tell me I am crazy, unwilling to accept a buyer for Brentwood, just four miles from my office, and with average home prices far higher than those in my area – but staying true to my goals and business model has always been one of my strongest attributes.

I leave you with three important messages:

First and foremost, adversity is a golden opportunity… and we should all welcome golden opportunities. They will keep you motivated, inspired, and uncomfortable enough to always keep fighting.

Second, define your goals. Know what you want and always work to achieve those targets. Be creative, and think outside of the box to provide solutions to problems.

Finally, stick to your business model. For me, I wanted to be a big frog in a small pond and I accomplished it. I have created a high quality of life and I'm now recognized as a true market expert… all while barely leaving my office.

Adversity is a gift, one you should search for and welcome in with open arms. Joyce Meyer said, "The eagle has no fear of adversity. We need to be like the eagle and have a fearless spirit of a conqueror." I hope the same is true for you. I have stood for adversity throughout my career. In some respects, I feel as if it is my **destiny**. I build on it, enjoy it, and allow it to be my greatest motivator.

ABOUT GEORGE

George Chung is Mar Vista, California's leading authority on real estate in the 90066 zip code. An energetic and insightful real estate broker, as well as a neighborhood advocate, he has the wonderful ability to inspire people to embrace their adversity and use it to propel them to success. He is also a commercially successful actor having been featured in *M*A*S*H, Baa Baa Black Sheep, LOST, SEARCH, ALIAS, West Wing,* and *Dark Blue.* George graduated from UCLA where he received his M.B.A and B.S in Engineering. He has lived in Seoul Korea, Tokyo Japan, and Southern California. He has been the past President of the United Multiple Listing Service, and for the past 42 years, a leading authority in the area of real estate marketing and deal-making in 90066 and has door knocked over one million homes in Mar Vista. As a result of his work with Bob Proctor, Mary Morrissey, and Jack Canfield, George developed a real estate program that incorporates the use of Thinking Into Results and Dream Building for real estate agents who want to develop their potential and personal effectiveness.

A STORY OF TRIUMPH – CAN I MAKE THE DISTANCE?

By Barry Hochstein

While I've had a good life, it has been fraught with many trials and challenges to overcome. When I say a good life, I mean I've never gone without a roof over my head, never known starvation, and never was so sick that I was 'Knockin' On Heaven's Door'.

I grew up in a large, extended Catholic family, where several aunts and great-aunts were nuns, and there was always a moderate expectation that I might be a priest one day. From serving as an altar boy, and then the church organist, I was always attending church for one function or another. As an organist, it also brought me to the big events – weddings and funerals. As a young high school student, it was always a thrill to perform at large weddings, with invitations to the rehearsals and associated parties. Funerals were more somber, but still a community event nonetheless.

What I gained from my upbringing was a deep belief that there was a God, a higher power that could be prayed to, and could be prayed to for others. I remember as a young child enjoying the colour pictures in our large family Bible, and reading some of the stories of the more famous characters, like Samson, Moses and David. My beliefs ran deep, supported by the extended family's commitment to serve in many capacities within the church. This would one day become critical to my very life.

There have been many "meteorites" as I call them, uninvited catastrophes and traumas in my life that come seemingly out of nowhere. Some people suggest we invite certain events into our life, which may be true when it comes to our thoughts but there are also the consequences of other peoples' actions, to which I have been subject, a little too often I sometimes think. Maybe God knows a little more than I do, just maybe…

The most significant triumph I experienced was the most recent in my life. After several physical traumas – a painful tooth extraction and three bad falls on ice whereon I hit so hard that I incurred a concussion, a neck injury and knocked out a tooth – I continued to suffer from extreme headaches. I am no stranger to headaches, from an offshore rig blowout in the 1980's, to three major motor vehicle accidents, each of which should have killed me, and the many other challenges the stress of life can throw at us.

For the last two and a half years I searched out every form of remedy I could possibly find to alleviate my headaches. The only relief was a mild narcotic painkiller, but at the very least, it worked, and the pain could be managed. I could carry on a degree of a life, work, and help family, but mostly, the headaches occurred every day.

I spent three additional weeks at the Hippocrates Health Institute, learning about healing techniques and how to maximize my immune system. I saw doctors, neurosurgeons, chiropractors, NUCCA chiropractors, orthotic specialists, a TMJ specialist (Temporomandibular Joint – the hinge of the jawbone impacted in one whiplash accident), used acupuncture, Chinese and First Nation traditional medicines, energy healing, essential oils, and the list goes on. I had the admonition given to me that I needed to do absolutely everything in my power to heal, and get on with my life.

I knew that every one of the fore-mentioned big accidents could have taken my life. Even under similar weather conditions where I rolled my truck four and three-quarter times, at 'warp' (110km/hr.), other individuals were not so fortunate, I walked away, many others died. I can only ascribe this to a belief that when God calls you, you go, but if he wants you to stay, you stay. This knowledge helps me and other accident survivors understand that you are not always singled out as someone special, but rather, your work here is not done, and there are others you have yet to help or things that need to be completed.

I have seen so many family and friends die 'early'. Cancer, alcoholism, heart attacks, drug addictions and despondency have taken many of my extended family 'before their time'. Not fully understanding, the best I could do was cope with my grief, and the grief of those around me. But I did learn one lesson in this facet of life, and death. It came quite unexpectedly from a *Reader's Digest* Humour in Uniform joke I had read many years ago. I never kept the page, but the gist of it was as follows: "A buck private was just finished military boot camp, and was getting ready to load his gear on the bus leaving after several hellish weeks. His tough old sergeant walked up to him and exclaimed 'I suppose when I die you'll probably come spit on my grave'. The private looked quietly at him and answered, 'No sir. I promised myself that when I left this man's army I would never stand in line again.'"

From this humour came a corollary that we only grieve for the people we love. We don't grieve for people we don't like, like the mean old sergeant. We can read through most obituaries calmly and without feeling. This, to me, had a deep impact – we only grieve for people we really love, therefore grief is nothing but an expression of profound love, and is part of a loving relationship.

I knew deep inside me that God preserved my life through all these painful events for a purpose, known only to Him, but hopefully one day I would learn too. So I kept on "keeping on," as they say.

After two and a half years, my pain and headaches were becoming a burden, and a line I remember from previous incidents came back to me – "death would be a sweet release." I knew I was reaching the end of my physical, mental and spiritual strength, and I needed more than I could do myself. In retrospect, at that point I had done literally everything I could possibly think of to do on my own. Now I needed help beyond what the world could offer, or the remaining time looked awfully bleak with a life of continuing pain.

In the midst of all this I began studying online from great inspirational motivational speakers such as Mary Morrissey, whose online webinars led me to Bob Proctor and Sandy Gallagher. I studied books from the greatest authors on the subject of inspiration – Norman Vincent Peale, Zig Ziglar, Dale Carnegie, among so many other great leaders in this field. The next steps were all part of a miracle beginning to form.

My wife, Janet, loves learning from the positive motivational speakers and teachers, and while listening to one speaker, an ad popped up about a big event that could change lives! Without reading the fine print, she filled in the online form for more information. Now, you have to know my wife. She loves quietly learning in her own space, but when she discovered that the email reply to her information query would result in someone calling, she almost panicked. But, she had hit the button, so she waited for the call. Two days later, she told the person on the phone who was following up with her online request, that she called for information for her husband, and he didn't even know about it!

We discovered that a major event was happening three thousand kilometers away, halfway across Canada in Toronto, Ontario, that lasted for six full days. The cost was seemingly prohibitive, and in US dollars, when the exchange rate was more than a full thirty per cent difference from our dollar.

I made a decision.

I was going to go, and I wanted my wife to travel with me. I did not want to be alone, and if my pain got so bad, I knew her comfort could always bring me back. Without hesitation, I sold my most valuable musical instrument. As a keyboard artist, I had several different instruments at home which I had used in public performances over the last 12 years, having played for over 50 years, starting when I was nine years old. I knew which could sell the fastest, and gain me the needed funds. I sold my beautiful Steinway grand piano.

I called the dealer that had last serviced it, and they were very interested, as they knew its condition and market value. They agreed over the phone that very same day. I drove an hour the next day to solidify the deal, and within a week, the piano was gone, and the much needed funds arrived shortly thereafter, and in time to attend the event. All this, and in a market in our province that severely depressed economically! Someone with more influence than me was helping.

I still had my headaches. I always rated the pain on a scale of zero to ten. "Tens" were commonplace for me, especially if I was negligent in taking my medications on time, or I hoped I could meditate the pain down (which sometimes worked from the self-hypno-therapy I had learned at pain clinics). The headaches were still hitting tens every day. Some days the pain brought me to tears, over and over again. Death was still looking like a sweet release. Nonetheless I booked my flight and hotel, and paid in full the cost of this major event in Toronto. I needed something more. I needed hope. Despair wasn't working.

My wife and I signed up for, and watched a three-day online streaming event, preparatory to the one I was interested in. Throughout the event I was hit with massive headaches, and spent most of my time medicated, lying on a bed, trying my best to listen, but having to admit I was missing most of what I was hearing.

As spring came early in the mountains where we live, my wife and I moved downstairs to the floor level where we had a spare bedroom. I remember very clearly that last night, lying in bed next to the window to take advantage of the cool evening air, exhausted from the pain, as we both went to sleep.

We had been asleep for about an hour, when I felt a brief touch on the back of my neck. I was lying facing my wife, but when I opened my eyes, she was sleeping turned away from me. I awoke her and asked if she had wanted something, having felt a touch on the back of my neck. She said "No."

The hair on the back of my neck stood straight up. As I write, I listen to music – rock 'n roll, country, classics, but as I write this paragraph the song "Praise to the Lord" is playing. Coincidence? I don't think so.

In my joy, I knew there was only one other person who could do such a thing. It hadn't been part of a dream, but was a real, physical, yet light touch of a hand on the back of my neck, where the source of my pain had originated. There is only one person I know that can appear, do such miracles, and leave quietly, and have the power to affect such a miracle.

My wife's prayers were answered that night. The source of my pain subsided instantly. We went to the event in Toronto, and for that week, the miracle continued.

Although our funds were insufficient for both of us to attend the event, the Matrixx, I had a deep, sincere, dream in my heart that I wanted her to attend with me. She agreed to travel with me, and spend her days in the hotel room doing cross-stitch and other sewing projects… so we left, and she came with me.

The first day was a Sunday. I met the event leaders, Bob Proctor and Sandy Gallagher in the event, and mentioned to them I had a story to share with them. They both agreed (amazing, as they are always SO busy, and we were told not to bother them with questions, as they needed their rest between sessions). But this wasn't a question. This was the story of how I made it to their event, and they agreed to meet with me. I texted my wife to hurry down from the hotel room and join me during the break, when I would be meeting with them.

She came straight down, and we were ushered into the nearby 'green room' where the event leaders refresh and rest between sessions. There were just the four of us there that Sunday afternoon, resting in large leather chairs. I was so excited to share the triumph I had just getting to the event, and the miracle that allowed me to fully participate, for the most part, without the mind-numbing narcotics that sometimes limit my creative cognitive abilities.

They had already heard the story of how I had been successful in selling my piano to afford to attend, which to me, wasn't really a sacrifice at all. I then shared the healing miracle I recently experienced, and how I needed hope and new opportunities. They first asked how I was enjoying the event, and I shared my truthful enthusiasm. Bob then turned to my wife and asked her how she was enjoying the event. Sensing her embarrassment, I interjected, and told Bob that unfortunately, I only had *one piano* to sell. He looked at Sandy. Sandy looked at Bob.

Bob said, "Well, she's in now!" Bob gave Sandy one look, and she jumped up and went outside to the event organizers who "made it so!" When Sandy returned in a couple of minutes, and in near tears, I expressed my heartfelt gratitude to the both of them.

Despite not being sure if I could go the distance or for how long, I made a decision to do something with my life, despite my painful circumstances. The consequences of that decision resulted in one miracle after another and not just for me – this was a major *triumph*!

Apart from simply attending the event, this was the sincerest desire of my heart for my wife to be on the same page as me! My wife and I strive to be on the same level in all aspects of our marriage, and this includes learning, reading, and attending events together. After raising five children, we now have time to get to really know each other and grow together for the second half of our lives.

Bob and Sandy made my deepest dream come true. Janet could attend and learn with me, and I wouldn't be 'ahead' of her in the knowledge and wisdom I would have gained on my own; rather, we were now together in the event, an event that would change both our lives, and help me rebuild my life. A higher power had intervened. I hadn't expected or even hoped for such a miracle, but it happened!

My new **destiny** lay just ahead of me.

About Barry

Married with five children, Barry has a passion for music and as a keyboard artist, plays classic rock 'n roll. Barry has authored and edited different publications for First Nations in Canada. An accomplished speaker, Barry has shared his expertise with thousands of conference attendees. Through these experiences, Barry has been challenged with the traumas from a rig blowout and three serious car accidents. A passionate and religious man, he ascribes his ongoing survival to God and His tender mercies, supported by friends and family. His story is intended to inspire, and help others find their God-given destinies, despite challenges.

DANCING IN THE DARK

BY MAY BARNES

Words, even those special words, often fall short of describing to others your experiences and feelings while living life on top of the world. For me, I found myself on top of the world when I met the man of my dreams, the love of my life. It was in that moment my life changed forever.

A very dear girlfriend invited me to an awards event. After multiple excuses and fielding much hesitation, she insisted I join her. It was a Black Tie evening, and I found the perfect gown in my closet. I applied makeup, and headed out for the evening, clad in a lovely dress. The event was to be held in the downtown area of our City. Hurry was not on my agenda, so it was no surprise dinner was over when I finally arrived. Lucky for me, the balance of the evening of dancing and socializing remained.

My friend introduced me to those at our table. We all participated in some small talk and got to know one another. One of the gentlemen at the table, a wonderfully handsome man, was doing his best to win over the favour of my best friend. Sadly, for him, she was not at all interested, as she had her sights elsewhere. By the end of the evening, he and I had chatted a bit and danced through many songs. At the end of the evening, it seemed as if we knew very little about one another, but there was an unspoken magic that was present between us. As we bid our farewells, I knew with certainty I would see this wonderful gentleman again. I looked forward to that meeting with great anticipation.

That was the prelude to a wonderful love story. A few days after the party, Jim called me and asked me to dinner. We both enjoyed dancing, and agreed to meet at a restaurant with a dance floor. After dinner and dancing, we went on a long stroll along the canal. It was a night to remember. Isn't it wonderful to relive all those wonderful times in our lives that brought us joy and contentment? We both knew that date was the beginning of a wonderful love story. From that night on, we spent as much time as we could together, enjoying our many common traits and getting to know the beauty of one another. Within a very short period of time, we decided to marry. We were both on top of the world.

Fairy tales do exist and I feel blessed to have had the experience of living one. Although love is an emotion that cannot be easily explained, it certainly is the planted seed that harvests many other emotions. When trying to explain these feelings aloud, it's hard to transform all those wonderful emotions into words. But I know firsthand that love is the most freeing experience there is. Opening up emotionally reveals a side of you that you might have never known existed. No flowery adjectives can express that moment when you look into someone's eyes and feel real love. But when you see it, you know it to be true.

Jim and I shared a one of a kind relationship. We felt blessed to have found one another. Each day grew better than the next. Our respect and constant conversation provided a life of true bliss. We were best friends, and there was no better fit for each of us. We took time apart to enjoy personal growth, but always returned home, knowing that our collective moments together meant the most.

What made me entitle this relationship? I am sure the words above give you a glimpse of the treasure I possessed. I often reference Oscar Wilde's quote: "Never love anybody who treats you like you are ordinary!" Well, let me tell you that was never the case with us – we both viewed one another as extraordinary and a true gift.

What a joy to know that you each would trade anything just to be together. We could talk about anything and everything. Kisses were lavish and often unexpected. We always exchanged sweet words, mostly "I love you." We would do anything to make the other happy, and our lengthy time together felt like mere moments. These are just some of the ways I would describe our love. Our time together was exciting, filled with love, joy, laughter, and lots of spontaneity. We both worked outside the home and usually not a week would pass where I would not receive that call around the noon hour asking for an impromptu lunch date filled with good food, wine, and great company.

Those calls and lunches brought great joy to me. Jim would regularly send me flowers, which would bring a smile to my face. But the truth is when you're riding the high of love, your smile always meets your ears. Suffice to say with all the foregoing, we were each other's everything. We danced in the foyer of our home like it was our own special dance floor. Our children would often comment that we are the only two they knew who could have a party and invite nobody.

We were both very fortunate to share the same activities like skiing, golf, water sports, roller blading, gardening, and attending hockey games. We had many years of enjoyment with hopes and conversations about growing old together, reminiscing about our past while sitting in our rocking chairs, still enjoying our glass of wine and laughing together. It certainly was our dream life and one that we were both looking forward to.

Well as they say, the best-laid plans sometimes don't materialize. We both enjoyed good health, rarely if ever sick. We remained very active, ate well, and were non-smokers. We made sure we had regular medical checkups, so it would seem that all bases were properly covered. Sadly, not so.

Jim hadn't felt well for a short time. This was out of the ordinary for him, so I suggested he visit the doctor. A few investigative appointments with medical tests followed. Then, the physician called and asked him to come in. He suggested I come with him, which I did. The doctor was concerned, and referred us to an Oncology Urologist. That referral was heart breaking for me, but Jim felt different. He was an eternal optimist and said, "We will just wait and see." We spent a very bizarre weekend together. I assumed the worst; Jim didn't worry at all. In fact, he wanted to go to dinner after the appointment. We met with the Oncologist the following Friday. While Jim wasn't worried, I worried enough for both of us.

On the following Friday, we learned that he had a rare type of cancer, usually prevalent in younger people and rarely growing in soft tissue. The diagnosis was devastating. The treating doctor presented the potential treatments options. We took some time to think about what we might do.

Without question, my first statement to the love of my life was we would do whatever he so chose. We could fight hard, or just enjoy whatever time we had left together. As I knew he would, Jim decided to fight. He chose a combination of traditional and alternative medicine. Although a serious situation, there were many chuckles along that way. The alternative medicine required brewing a special tea in a special brewer that was so obnoxious in odor that I would brew it in the garage. He would sigh, and faithfully drink it. Trust me when I tell you it looked and smelled like tar.

Since he was the forever optimist, Jim asked that I not share the severity of his illness with friends or family. When your best buddy asks you to do something that will ease his situation under such terrible circumstances, you just do it. I travelled with him to hospital visits, surgery, and various treatments. It was a very lonely voyage for me, as I had no shoulder to rest on when times got tough… and they did. There was only ten precious months from date of diagnosis to death. It was a real roller coaster ride. Our two youngest children were still at home, requiring the usual attention and love from their mother and father. There were many days where I felt like a cat on a tin roof, running from activity to activity to doctor's appointment. It wasn't easy to keep everything afloat.

Through the first several months of his treatment, we were still able to enjoy a somewhat subdued version of our wonderful happy times together. We made the best of every minute of every day. My sweetheart, even sick as he was, did not want me to have a 50th Birthday without a celebration. He set aside his pain and suffering to plan a beautiful party for me. We invited family and friends and shared stories and exchanged love deep into the evening.

Five months into the treatment, we did not see any hopeful results, so the doctor recommended surgery, with great hopes of success. I remained a strong and loving spouse, but that decision was left with him. He decided to have the surgery, which proved to be very hard on him. In the recovery room, he left us for a couple of minutes, and returned to describe something magnificent to me. He shared a vision of the gates of Heaven, whites like you have never seen. He informed me of the peace and tranquility we don't experience here on earth.

A couple of months of suffering followed and the fall months were not kind months to Jim and his illness. He went from a strapping 6'2" absolutely stunning looking man to a skeleton. His attitude remained positive. If he could take in even a tablespoon of nourishment, he considered it a great day and a step in the right direction. I stayed with Jim at the hospital day and night, only leaving his side a few times a week for a quick run to clear my mind. In the wee hours of the morning on Sunday before his death, Jim said he needed to talk. This was a conversation nobody wants to have or hear. We chatted and he told me that he had been spending a great deal of time in deep thought. He said even if he suffered for another few months, he did not see wellness at the other end of this challenge. He shared with me he would like to die and move on to the next part of his journey. To say I was in shock would be putting it mildly, but I had given him my word. I told him I would support him. His concern was still for me and not himself, but he wanted to make sure I would be all right. We began calling family and friends. He spent that Sunday saying his goodbyes to them. Talk about strength on everyone's part. Tragically, my treasured life partner and best friend died around 7:00PM the following day.

It was very difficult for his family and friends, given the lack of information regarding his condition. I respected Jim's wish to keep quiet the seriousness of his diagnosis. Right or wrong, I respected his wish. I always say to my children, "You must be your word. If you are not your word, you are not authentic." His death was a terrible shock to many. They were deeply hurt and blamed me for not sharing the details of Jim's condition.

I began a journey of melancholy. I had received little support throughout his illness and death. I now had even less. I didn't even have the opportunity to celebrate his beautiful life. His family and friends questioned many of my actions and decisions. Love turned to hate, feuds ensued and my world began to disintegrate one little piece at a time.

Blended families can be challenging at even the best of times. But with the death of a loved one, these small issues can grow to be a giant with little remedies available to those involved. Jim lived the life of a millionaire, so it didn't surprise me that folks questioned my honesty regarding funds. Offshore accounts with zero balances were thought to contain millions. Jim was an entrepreneur at heart and started many businesses – one he even started shortly before his diagnosis. I helped to fund the endeavour, and I collapsed all my retirement funds to provide the money for him. He was a success and I had no reason to believe the same would not be true this time around. But his illness did not allow that. It's tough when people judge and blame you without having all the facts.

After his death, I faced insurmountable challenges. I had put my own business on hold to become his primary care giver, almost a necessity these days if anyone is familiar with the Canadian Health Care System. Again, without being able to share with my clients the 'why' behind my absence, many of my clients went elsewhere. I had to start from ground zero when I resumed my business. Jim left me with a six-figure debt, and a promise to repay everyone. I intended to keep this promise, but it required some major changes in my lifestyle. This is not easy to explain to his children. I had been divorced by his entire world, as a feeling of loneliness, sadness, fatigue, fear, incapability, lack of self-confidence, self-image and self-esteem began to grow and take over my world. I lost myself for a bit of time, but I quickly realized I could not continue down that path. I resided in my own world of grief.

My entire relationship was an experience of terrific love, loss, death, rebirth and a return to merriment. I shared this story with you to set the stage for what I believe was a basket of true blessings I found along the way to reconnecting to the woman I was when experiencing love with my treasured partner such as pure, lustful, joyous, adoring, romantic, boundless, deep, and surprising. Magic existed in his eyes, and his energy would light up a room. In his arms I had no fears.

So what steps did I take to reengage with life? None at first. I wondered if I might just wallow in self-pity. I became the world's best procrastinator, not having had much time to grieve and not really being in touch with reality. I felt like 'it's ok, everything will be ok'. Then reality set in, like mortgage payments, back taxes, education expenses, living expenses, and rebuilding my business. I sat down and put together a plan I thought could take me from my quite undesirable financial situation to the light at the end of the tunnel.

What followed were major changes for not only myself, but also the children. It was time to sell the house, a travesty, because it was the most beautiful home on the waterfront. The children loved it, as it was a home with many exquisite memories for everyone. I needed every penny from the sale of the home, so I sold the home myself without a realtor. Finding a new home was not easy. I hadn't any money saved for a down payment, and I wasn't working at the time. At this point I was looking for some magic to drop from the sky. We managed to find a home, and I sold some stock in a company for the down payment. I even found a lender who believed in me and loaned me the additional money needed. That home did not last long, as I was overwhelmed with unexpected outstanding debts. In response, I sold that home after living there for less than one year. We rented furnished facilities while I got back to where I had been before the day of Jim's diagnosis.

I literally had to rebuild our lives in every way, not just financially, but emotionally and physically. Jim's death took a toll on my physical being and ability to rebuild my lost relationships. Although there is sadness in Jim's death, I learned a lot from it. I was able to return to merriment through my faith and belief in myself. I realized I was in control of my own results, my happiness, my health and every aspect of my daily life, no matter what the circumstances. To allow others to dictate my results is in and of itself a travesty that should never be given to anyone.

I became the owner of my every day. Jim left with me treasured words from his deathbed. I try to live these words each and every day. He made me promise him I would live every day to the fullest and never pass up an opportunity for happiness. I knew I couldn't do that while living in a state of pity and victimhood? It could not happen.

In growing together and trying to live with our great loss as a family, we would start each day by writing down ten things for which we were grateful. Since we were rebuilding, they need not be big things, just small details that could put us in a state of gratitude and provide us with a wonderful attitude to start the day. We also sent love to those who bothered us. Sounds simple, but it took an open mind and heart to make that part of our daily routine. We noticed as our gratitude increased, our life improved. A check would arrive out of the blue, we'd receive an invitation to dinner with new friends, or we'd enjoy a beautiful sunset or long walk as a family. Before we knew it, life was getting brighter and brighter every day.

I still enjoyed the same love with which I started my life. It never left us, it just appeared in a different form. Through tenacity, a belief in myself, and the will to face struggles with a positive attitude, I have not only come out as a survivor, but also as a winner. I learned plenty of lessons the hard way, but today I am a wonderfully, happy, healthy, successful businesswoman with a tremendous life ahead of me.

I do enjoy every minute of every day and never pass up an opportunity for happiness. It has become a way of life for me. When troubles land on your doorstep, I suggest you do the same. Where there is love there is life. That will always remain with you. Trust yourself in any situation, believe that you are a survivor, send kindness each day to those that bother you, and remember to always start your days with five minutes of quiet time while asking for guidance for the day ahead. Combine these with a positive and happy attitude. These simple yet powerful steps will help you to overcome the trials and tribulations life often puts in your path. Follow your own insight and know that your gut instinct is strong. The heart sees what's invisible to the eyes. Everything we will ever need to surmount the biggest challenge or sorrow we may face lies within us.

Stories of destinies are many and plentiful, each with its touch of pain and its touch of pure joy. When we are truly present each day and live that day to the fullest, we can often fall into a sense of feeling that destiny will only bring us joy and that is a great way to spend each 24 hours we are given to enjoy. My wonderful loving father used to remind me today, is the tomorrow you worried about yesterday. There is no need to worry about each day or the road you may have to travel to reach your glorious and amazing fulfilled destiny. Living in the ocean of truth each day, being mindful of being calm and in control of you at all times and remembering to think your way through each day, will allow you to hold your head high and have your heart full of joy through any and all tragedies or travesties or seemingly tough or big decisions that may be presented to you. Believe in you, believe in the power of your thoughts and know that your **destiny** is dictated by you. As James Allen says in his book *As a Man Thinketh*, "Self-control is strength, Right Thought is Mastery and Calmness is Power – say unto your heart – Peace be still!" Wonderful words to take with you along your Destiny Journey.

Try to be mindful of only seeing through your sometimes self-centered eyes, with gratitude for all that is, take a moment and wonder what the other person who is experiencing this tragic situation is seeing from their eyes – are you seeing their pain, or only focused on your own? Always send love not daggers and love will be returned to you tenfold.

And don't ever forget to dance your way through life…

ABOUT MAY

May Barnes is a certified master life coach with over 30 years of experience in marketing, communications, sales and Human Resources. Her mission is to help people ignite the greatness within and she amplifies this goal through her work as a writer, and motivational speaker. May also specializes in success coaching for business and communications consulting. Active in her community, May volunteers at a local Nursing Home, she is also a member of a number of local charities. May also holds several designations within the Financial Services Industry, CHS, RHU, CLU. May is also a Certified Staging Professional enhancing living environments. May is a competitive Ballroom Dancer. She loves to spend as much time as possible with her four amazing children and her four beautiful grandchildren.

THE SECRET OF NUMBERS

BY ANDREA TONELLO

Italian tradition dictates the eldest son take charge of the family business when he reaches adulthood. No matter what family he's born to, his life plan is predetermined for him. The vocation may be different, but the tradition remains the same. A farmer's son becomes a farmer; a cobbler's boy becomes a cobbler; or, as in my family's case, a barber's son must fulfill his destiny of cutting hair as a career. Family tradition is so strong in my country that breaking out of the mold cast for you set down by the preceding generations is forbidden. In my childhood home in northern Italy's province of Vicenza, my family ardently clung to this idea. As a youngster, this never sat well with me because it afforded me no opportunity to choose a future of my own. Early on, I decided to cast off these restrictions and choose my own path.

Lesson #1 - Make your own way in life.

The day my favorite elementary school teacher asked the class what we wanted to be when we grew up, without hesitation I declared, "I want to be a lawyer." Perhaps it was my decisiveness or the defiant nature of my answer, but whatever it was, she encouraged me. "Bravo!" she said, clapping her hands. Learning of my ambition, my father dismissed it as a childhood fantasy since he'd been grooming me to be a barber all along. However, it wasn't a fantasy to me. **A still small voice, like a soft breeze, had whispered to me.**

The day I decided to be a lawyer, the seed of that aspiration firmly planted itself in my mind. The idea took root and the fantasy flashed pictures nonstop in my mind. In my waking hours, I daydreamed about how it would feel and what it would be like. At night my dreams revealed a grown up me wearing suits and ties, arguing cases before a judge and jury and celebrating with my clients after winning their cases in court. The idea excited my seven year old self, and the more I focused on it, the more it grew into a burning desire. From that young age, my life's mission became one of helping people to solve their legal problems.

As a teenager, the time had come for high school. My father became enraged when he learned of my plans to enroll. "Your grandfather is turning over in his grave!" he declared, "Your obligation is to your family, not to your own selfish wants. You must become a barber. School is unnecessary."

"I'm going to be an attorney," I said defiantly. Heated arguments erupted around the dinner table over plates of pasta. Everyone had an opinion about my future, and each did their part to change my mind. But I would hear nothing of their pleas, instead I held my ground. My determination was such that no amount of anger or pleading could dissuade me from pursuing my dream. Eventually, my father finally gave in, and I enrolled in high school. The voice inside me cheered!

Upon graduating from high school, once again, he attempted to assert his control over my future. "You've gotten very smart in the last five years," he said, attempting to approach me with calm emotion, "now you must run the barbershop." It felt like déjà vu. Why did he not respect my desire to pursue a future of my own choosing? Never being one to trade my happiness for the sake of keeping the family peace, I mustered all my courage and confronted him. "No!" I commanded adamantly, "It's too late. I've already enrolled in and paid tuition for Law School. I'm going with or without your blessing." Any further arguments I dismissed with a flick of my wrist. His shoulders shrugged when he realized that he had been whipped. At long last, he gave up the fight, and blessed me in the pursuit of my lifelong dream.

Lesson #2 - Hold fast to your dream no matter what.

Looking back on that time, I realize now that being a barber would have made me miserable. I have nothing against barbers, we all need them, but

I'd probably stab someone with a pair of scissors. Because I stood up to my father and fought for myself, I passed through an invisible barrier from boyhood to stand on the other side as a powerful man. A new understanding of my own power began to emerge from this rite of passage. Self-determination and self-direction were two important traits I acquired all those years ago when I stood up for myself. More importantly, the realization that having a dream and making the decision to keep it alive over a sustained period of time served me well to bring my goal into reality.

After law school, I received an apprenticeship as a civil servant in Italy's National Archives. My first assignment was to move the library's contents from its original location to a new home. For 12 months, I removed books from their shelves and wiped them clean before boxing them up and transferring them to their new home in a villa of extraordinary beauty. The hours were long and tedious, but I didn't mind. In fact, just being in the presence of those books inspired me. Oftentimes, I'd leaf through pages and read the writings of classical authors such as Seneca and Marcus Aurelius as well as those of contemporary writers. Their teachings on philosophy, life, love, happiness and an individual's life purpose stirred something deep within me. I experienced the beginnings of an awakening. Was I truly living up to my fullest potential? I'd take these books home and read them into the wee hours, pondering their ancient wisdom. **There was that voice in my head again, but what was it saying?**

My good fortune continued when the owner of a private law firm in Vincenza saw potential in me, and gave me my first real job even though I hadn't yet completed my law school course work. Of course, I had to balance my work load with my school, but eventually I graduated and passed the bar. All I could think about was how grateful I felt for having finally achieved my dream.

My job at the law firm continued once I was a full-fledged attorney, and the owner relied on me more and more. One day, when he was running late, he asked me to take his place in an appointment, and I agreed. The moment the client, Michela, walked into the office, I fell madly in love with her. The way she reached out her hand to shake mine, the beautiful smile she flashed me when she introduced herself and the radiance her skin shone when the light caught it captivated me. Sparks flew between us, and we soon began dating; eventually we married.

For the next few years, life progressed in an upward spiral, each milestone surpassing the last. By the age of 27, I had built my own financially successful law firm, married the love of my life and one year later welcomed our daughter, Arianna, into the world. Despite having what appeared to be a perfect life, a feeling of discontent creeped into my subconscious, zapping joy from my life. The time had come to look beyond my original dream and find a new one. Where should I start? Introspection provided me with the answer I sought – find happiness and deeper meaning in life. I reflected on the time when I was the happiest in my life. The voice inside yelled too loudly for me to ignore any longer.

Lesson #3 - Recreate yourself when the compulsion seizes you.

My mind returned to the happiness I felt turning the pages of those old books, mulling over their teachings, and reflecting on their wisdom. Seeking answers to life's bigger questions was the most fulfilling period in my life. A rekindled zest for life seized me, fanning a flame within me to pursue this kind of knowledge again. A curiosity led me to discover modern day thought leaders such as Bob Proctor, Deepak Chopra, the Dalai Lama among others. These teachers had wisdom and were still alive. I bought their books and devoured them, highlighting, underlining and rereading every chapter. I made it my goal to have them as mentors.

Before stumbling upon these teachings, I had never heard the term 'Personal Development' even though I had been unconsciously practicing it for years. Until that point I had strived with a dogged determination to create a successful life by putting all my effort on my external environment. I had been focused on the visible world outside of myself. However the advice of these teachers directed me to turn my focus inward to the invisible side of myself, the universe of thought and spirit heretofore unexplored consciously. Now I had the means to identify things that I had only previously had a feeling about although I always knew they were there. Pieces to a puzzle began falling in place. **"Pay attention," the voice said.**

Lesson #4 - Seek the help of mentors.

The next phase of my journey took me to transformational seminars where I met likeminded people all interested in personal growth. At one particular event in Milan, a woman took the stage and spoke of a method of reading numbers of people's birth dates and interpreting them by means of an ancient process. Her name was Monika Ben Thabetova. So impressed, I found her in the lobby during a break and asked to speak to her further about her numbers system. Unfortunately, there wasn't enough time at the seminar to meet, but she agreed to schedule a Skype call in the coming days. During our session, she read the significance of my birthdate numbers, telling me things about myself no one else knew. She told me I was a teacher, and my destiny was to write books and become a motivational speaker. "You know this is true if you'd tune in to the voice inside." This took me by surprise. How did she know about that voice? Her words rang true and gave me a new perspective on my life's mission, but how would I move forward?

I asked for Monika's help. If I was to walk a new spiritual path, I would need assistance and she agreed to help me. Once a month, we hiked majestic mountain trails above Lake Como and talked about life and our destinies. Over time, she pulled back the veil that shrouded the secret of numbers and their special energy. I began to study and understand the amazing power of this tool. "Everything is a number," she explained, "and each has its own significance in our lives that is beyond our comprehension." In a flash, the voice echoed in my head, telling me to bring the secret of numbers to the world. When I told her about it, she nodded knowingly, "We are meant to work together."

A new meaning for my life emerged, but to get the word out on a grand scale, I would need to enlist the help of people who had a global following. Before I begun to study personal development material, I would have been paralyzed at not knowing how or where to begin. But now I knew as long as I had a clear vision of my goal, the way would be shown.

During an online class hosted by Bob Proctor, he had a guest, *New York Times* Best-selling author, Peggy McColl, who I somehow knew would play a role in helping us launch *The Secret of Numbers*. Her specialty is coaching people to launch their books, make them best-sellers and building businesses around their concepts.

Currently, Monika and I are working to bring our book, online classes and live seminars to life with the help of Bob & Peggy. These two mentors are beacons of hope transmitting a message that anyone can change the world if they can dream it and have the guts to bring it into reality.

Since embarking on my new mission, the voice in my head has gone silent. It isn't as though it's gone away or left my head, but rather, since my life's purpose and my intuition are now in alignment, I believe the two voices have merged and are now one. My **destiny** will be fulfilled.

In conclusion, my story wouldn't be complete without thanking my wife, my daughter and our dog for embracing my desire to be more. To Monika, who has entrusted me to nurture her dream as if it were my own and, of course, my father the barber and my mother, without whom I never would have had the courage to dare to grow into the man I am today.

If you want to find out how this story continues visit the website www.thesecretofnumbers.com

ABOUT ANDREA

Andrea Tonello was born in Italy in 1975, he graduated in Law at the University of Bologna. He is the founder of the Law Firm Tonello that, with great success, helps companies solve their problems. Since 2014 collaborates together with Monika Ben Thabetova and spreads the message contained in the book *The Secret of Numbers*, of which he is co-author. Andrea holds live courses on personal and spiritual growth with which it contributes and helps people to have a new awareness of who they really are. The acquired knowledge, along with the informations transmitted and the tools, facilitate the transformation process necessary to achieve harmony and inner peace that leads people to live their life with more happiness!

A PUPPY AND A PURPOSE

BY RICCI REARDIN MILLS AND MARCO MILLS

Growing up, I was obsessed with trying to figure out my destiny. What was I meant to do with my life? What was I supposed to be? I spent hours upon hours wondering and worrying about this. For a while I dreamt about being an artist, a doctor, a soccer player, a film producer (it's pretty obvious for which one of these options my parents were rooting). How was I supposed to choose? How was I supposed to know what I really wanted? What if I made a mistake and picked the wrong thing? The older I got, the more logic told me I should be getting closer to realizing my destiny; instead it felt like it was getting further and further away from me. I feared I would live my life never knowing my purpose. Then one day, my destiny showed up in the way I least expected… in a puppy.

I never thought I would have a puppy. I never really cared about dogs. I thought they were dirty, unsanitary, annoying, and wasn't sure why people wanted them. I preferred a world without them but in a blink of an eye everything changed. I had a puppy. She was an adorable nine-week-old Yorkie Maltese mix that weighed a whopping two pounds. I named her Coconut. My husband Marco was elated. Living in Los Angeles together, he had grudgingly accepted a dog-less life soon after meeting me and couldn't believe we now had this adorable two-pound ball of fluff he got to train and mold. I didn't know what I was getting myself into but thankfully he grew up with dogs so I let him take complete control.

After having Coconut for three weeks Marco booked a trip home to Canada to visit his family. Panic began bubbling up in me as the days got closer to his departure. I didn't know how I was going to survive those two weeks alone with Coconut. She kept us up at night. She whined, cried and barked, had accidents all over the house, and chewed on every piece of once-decent furniture we owned. She attacked my ankles when I walked. I couldn't even wear socks anymore because she would chase me like a maniac! My world was completely changed, and I was not liking it. How did people live like this? In such chaos? Without getting any sleep? With not wearing socks anymore? How could one live with a smelly, wild animal living with them in their *home*, destroying (physically and emotionally) every sense of a normal, comfortable and easy life they once had? Did you know they don't understand how to walk on a leash? Or sit? Or to *not* bite your fingers off? You have to teach them – everything. This was madness… and now this was my life. Picking up poop and cleaning pee messes every day while listening to a soundtrack of constant barking, whining, and scratching. It was utter madness.

It was in these moments I completely understood why some owners would decide to give their pups up to shelters from sheer overwhelm, frustration, and a lack of not knowing what they were getting themselves into or what, if anything, they could do to fix it. I knew I was in way over my head but giving her up was never an option for me (although, I admit in my worst puppyhood moments I did let the thought temporarily flash in my mind). I made the decision to get her and I would be a responsible owner and care for her for her entire life. I simply accepted for the next twelve years or so, I would be miserable. That's truly how I thought it was going to be. I sincerely believed I had made the worst decision of my life getting her and I was angry with myself for getting caught up in the cuddly cute notion of having a puppy, and not being prepared for what was really in store.

Somehow, I survived those two weeks alone with her while Marco was away… barely. I counted down the seconds until I got to leave to pick Marco up from the airport so he could save me from this furry beast who had taken over my life, not allowing me any time to do anything because of the constant supervision, attention, and care she required. She drained me. My freedom had completely vanished. I was stressed out, completely overwhelmed, and exhausted. Even a quick trip to the supermarket had to be properly planned to correspond with her sleep and bathroom schedule. By schedule, I mean me guessing how long I could be out before her waking up, having an accident, eating it, ripping up my carpet and cushions, or anything else I cherished she could find before I could stop her.

The morning Marco was at the airport returning to L.A., I got a call from him two hours before he was scheduled to take off with news I never in a million years would have expected. The call would change everything – my whole life – as I knew it. Customs had denied him entry back into the United States. He didn't know if or when he'd be allowed back into the country. In other words, I was on my own. He wasn't coming home. This nightmare wasn't over, it was just beginning.

Along with trying to figure out how to get my husband back in the country while taking care of all his responsibilities here, and while learning how to live this different life apart from him long-term and simultaneously trying to understand why this was happening and why the universe was doing this... I had to figure out how to raise this puppy. It was her and me and we were on this journey together, whether we liked it or not (I'm pretty sure she was even less thrilled about it than I. Her trusted leader was gone, and she was stuck with the crazy lady who had no idea what she was doing).

I didn't know it at the time, but having this new puppy, and now being alone and having to raise her, turned out to be two of the most integral steps on this journey that would lead to me ultimately discovering my destiny.

When the initial shock of Marco not coming home began to wear off, I realized to keep my sanity (or what was left of it) and move forward, I had to get this puppy trained. I needed professional help NOW. I couldn't continue life like this – not with a husband stuck out of the country with some of the best lawyers telling us it would be years before he could possibly return. I wasn't going to accept their prognosis, just like I wasn't going to tolerate life with a misbehaved puppy growing into a worse-behaved dog because of a completely clueless owner.

I did what most first-time puppy owners do – I walked into the local big box pet store chain to check out their puppy training classes. I hated being in there. These big pet supply warehouses represented everything I detested in my previous non-dog life. They had a wretched smell that made me want to gag, they weren't especially welcoming, there were way too many out of control animals in there, and really, I didn't know what half the stuff in there was for and if I needed or would ever need it. (I hoped I wouldn't.) This was a foreign world of which I did not feel a part – nor did I want to feel a part. My skin itched and I had to constantly resist the urge to turn around and run out the door.

I walked over to the training area and studied their upcoming class schedule like I was solving a math problem: examining when the next puppy classes started, what days and times they were available, looking for that opening – that glimmer of hope – that there was soon an end to this life of disarray. Unfortunately, the closer I looked, that glimmer faded and the disappointment grew. The next class started in three weeks (three more weeks of living like this?) and all the weekly one-hour class times were during my work hours. Literally, there was not one single class I could make out of their full month of training classes offered. Not a person to easily give up, I rationed this wasn't the place I was 'meant' to take my puppy for training, and I moved on.

I drove straight to the next closest competing big box pet store chain to check out *their* training class schedule. This time I only had to wait two weeks to start, but again every class time offered, I had a conflict. What kind of a sick joke was this? What was I supposed to do? What about the people who worked long or weird hours from the 'norm' and couldn't make these class times? Were they just supposed to learn how to train their puppies themselves? Cause I did NOT have the time to search YouTube for Do-It-Yourself training tricks and then attempt to teach them to my pup. And let's get real: the probability of my puppy understanding training from me, Miss Never-had-a-dog-in-her-life, was pretty much a guaranteed failure.

Completely deflated, I retreated home and went straight to where I always went whenever I needed some quick help and guidance... Google. I began searching for "best dog trainers near me" and skimming through the related website results. The more I searched, the more discouraged I became. Not that I should judge a trainer's success by their website design, clearly those are two very different talents, but the ones I came across were so unimpressive and so amateur-looking, I worried that if their training was as good as their websites, I was in serious trouble. At the time, no one seemed impressive to me.

With one last desperate search in the Google box, something popped up that caught my eye: "drop-off dog training." I had never heard of that before. Interest peaked, I eagerly clicked on their website. I scanned and learned it was a Japanese-style dog training school where the dogs were trained during the day without the owners present. I didn't even know what Japanese-style dog training was, but the concept excited me and their website was one of the better ones I'd seen! I immediately called to set up an appointment to come in and learn more. To be honest, they couldn't have kept me from NOT showing up that day.

In a couple hours, I had my wild puppy in one arm (trying to wrestle with me and jump out of my grip, naturally) while the other arm drove 20 minutes to an area of town I had never been to before. My GPS took me to a plaza dedicated to Japanese businesses. The training facility I was looking for shared a space with a dog groomer. It was small and unimpressive, but seemed clean and didn't smell like dogs (huge bonus). What was impressive was who greeted me. This young, pretty, kind girl introduced herself as Ayumi, one of the trainers there, and invited me to take a seat. I was supposed to meet with another trainer, but last minute Ayumi was asked to fill in instead. I was destined to meet her. As she saw me struggle with my pup while attempting to have her sit still on my lap and not gnaw at my hands, she asked if it would be ok if she took her for me. I all but tossed Coconut to her. I'm sure she could see the mixed look of desperation and relief in my eyes as she scooped Coconut away from me and took over. I think Coconut and I both shared a mutual sigh of relief. I instantly felt a wave of comfort that this person knew exactly what she was doing and that I could trust her. And I could tell Coconut felt the same thing. Ayumi was so calm with a gentle confidence – so different from the high-energy, high-speaking trainers I had met before. I knew this is what we both needed. It just felt right.

By the following week I had Coconut signed up and was bringing her to all-day training classes two days a week. It was perfect – a dream come true, really. I could get a day to myself to run errands and get work done, and Coconut was in expert hands being watched, trained, and becoming a better mannered pup without me having to struggle to figure it out along with her. What could be better? In that moment, I was so grateful that my work schedule never allowed me the time to partake in those other training classes I was initially looking into. Clearly, I was meant to have found this new trainer Ayumi, who was about to change my entire relationship with my puppy forever.

As I started being shown what Coconut could learn and do, how to properly understand her and guide her, and how she would actually for the first time ever, respond when I asked her to do something, my world shifted. We were *communicating* – her and me. We understood each other. She *wanted* to know what I wanted from her. I couldn't believe it. Learning more about her and why she was acting in a certain way, and what she needed from me as her parent and leader, was the beginning to us forming this new understanding, new relationship, and new incredible bond I never ever knew was possible. As she got better, I got better, and as I got better, she got better. The regret and overwhelming feeling I had when she first came into my life morphed into this unconditional love and gratitude for her being in my life. I was the last person on earth who ever thought this might happen to. I went from wanting to give this dog away, to her becoming my best friend I didn't want to be apart from.

While this transformation was happening with Coconut and I, Marco and I were manifesting a miracle for his early return home to California. It happened. After four months of being stuck in Canada, Marco was finally back home with me – and now I was teaching *him* what to do and how to work with Coconut!

It was three months after his homecoming when the idea first struck me like lightening. Oprah calls it the "Aha" moment, but for me it was a full body shock. The strongest tingling sensation that started from my heart, spread to every part of my body, and made me freeze for probably a full five seconds. With the tingling was a deep knowingness, as if this idea of what I was supposed to do had always been with me, and everything I had been going through suddenly made sense – My destiny was to have gotten this puppy, to experience what it was like to raise a puppy as a brand new owner, on my own, so I could gain the insight as to what new owners really need. I started to realize how much more could be done for these owners. I needed to create a service business that would be their ultimate support system through the puppyhood experience. I would help make puppyhood easy for them. I needed to open my own puppy school and I knew that Coconut's trainer Ayumi was going to be my partner.

There were more owners like me out there – I know – I had found the online discussion groups! Owners like me who didn't know what to do, who had thought they had made the worst mistake getting a puppy, who were living in a world run by their dog, who didn't know where to turn. I knew I could provide them with a service that would help them and change their lives for the better. I had to help the owners.

This was crazy. I didn't even like dogs! I didn't like dog places! My old self and her views were fighting my new self and what I knew I had to do. If I didn't like what was out there, surely others didn't either. I would create a dog service with me as the customer in mind. A place that felt like an upscale, inviting home, that was calm and fresh, instead of a sterile cold warehouse with barking dogs, neon colors and cartoon dog cut-outs that smelled like one hundred unbathed dogs lived there. I would create a place I would actually want to leave my puppy, with people who felt like family that I trusted, with all the knowledge and guidance new owners needed. We would be their support group, we would train their puppies for them, and we would teach them what they needed to know. We would show them what to do. We would help build that incredible communication, bond and trust between them and their puppy that they probably never knew was possible. This place didn't exist, and I knew it had to.

I had many entrepreneurship ideas before. What was so different about this one? What set this idea apart? I kept asking myself as I questioned my sanity and the likeliness of this goal succeeding. The answer was crystal clear to me: this idea was different because it was meant for *others*. It was the first time I had gotten a vision of doing something that would impact other people so significantly, for which I was passionate. I had to do this for *them*.

With my new crazy idea, I set out to open the ultimate puppy training school and owner support center. First step: I had to tell Marco about it. This was not the first time he had to patiently listen to an out-there vision of mine, but when I saw his eyes light up as I described it to him, and felt his belief that he genuinely loved the concept, I was even more on fire with it. I enrolled him in this vision and he immediately agreed to help me make this happen.

Second step: with Marco now committed, we needed to enroll Ayumi – the puppy expert. If I was going to embark on this new insane venture in a field I only recently started learning about, she's the one person I could see doing this with us. I was so nervous asking her. It's like the entire future of this dream depended on her answer. Thankfully, and kind of to my surprise, she said she was on board! Things were getting real now. I was so far responsible for shifting the destinies of two other people. That's a lot of pressure. I couldn't let them down.

The third step: actually *doing* it and making this dream come to life. That was going to be a little more challenging.

To say I had absolutely no idea what I was doing or how I was going to do it (especially with an extremely limited budget) was an understatement. Fortunately, I didn't spend too much time dwelling on that. I was blissfully oblivious. I focused solely on my end vision and my burning desire to help other puppy owners out there. With this on the forefront of my mind and my dominant purpose every second of the day, somehow, through the help of what could only be greater powers, everything started coming together. Even when at first circumstances didn't appear to be in my favor – and oftentimes they didn't – everything that happened, negative or positive, all contributed to my dream manifesting into its physical form.

· · ·

With Marco and Ayumi now on this journey with me, we got to work. We picked the name, bought the domain (which was available!), opened an LLC, and began planning the entire puppy training program and exactly how we were going to help these owners. It was then time to find a designer to bring my brand and logo ideas to life.

For days I hunted, researched and emailed different designers and companies I thought might be able to build from my sketch, but nothing felt right. I questioned their ability to really produce on paper what was in my head. I was skeptical and felt unsure. I needed to step away for a moment to regroup and readjust my search process. I took a break to go to an appointment I had scheduled, and was greeted by my usual super friendly, talkative nurse who was excitedly chattering about her new home decoration store she was taking over and was getting ready to open. When I told her I was in the middle of trying to find a logo designer for my new business, she mentioned she had just gotten her logo designed and whipped out her phone to show it to me. I couldn't believe it – it was exactly the look and feel I was hoping to achieve with mine! I absolutely loved it! She told me the designer lived in the area and shared her contact information. When I got home, I emailed her immediately and she began working with my ideas right away. She got it – she got me, she got my vision. I was so relieved. I knew I was supposed to have met her. After a few revisions, we ended up with the most amazing logo for which I could have asked. I still smile every time I see it. My puppy school finally had an identity!

I soon learned, as it was repeatedly proven to me, when I set my intention of what I was determined to create, the universe completely took over. This idea was becoming its own energy field. It was taking on a life of its own... and it was my duty to guide it into its physical existence. We were committed to each other, and because of that, the most incredible things continued to happen.

Every single piece of furniture I liked and wanted for the puppy school, went on sale. So much so that I had purchased almost every item we needed before we had even found a location and signed a lease. My home started looking more like a warehouse than an apartment, but I didn't care. I didn't even attempt to hide anything or put them in storage – I wanted the piled-high cardboard boxes to be a constant reminder for me of what I was doing, and I needed them to be in my face as much as possible. These boxes needed their real home.

The biggest challenge turned out to be in securing a location. For almost two years, we were either rejected or beat out by another business, on multiple properties. We had even signed leases, and later lost them to other tenants. (Yes, this can actually happen – and did.) On two of the locations we were 'supposed' to get, we later discovered that on one, the new tenants ran into major construction issues, costing them hundreds of thousands in repairs they were responsible for. On the other one, a pipe burst completely flooding and forcing the newly renovated, recently moved in business to close down after only being open for two months. Had we of gotten either of these leases, we would have been sunk before even getting off the ground. Two of our biggest disappointments on this journey turned out to be two of the best things to happen to us.

When we finally found a lease on a place we loved AND got accepted, I was completely elated. Until then, there was a voice inside me whispering every now and then "what if this doesn't ever happen." Then it almost didn't. Suddenly, we were on the verge of losing this lease because of a permit issue with the city. They wanted $5000 and six months to present our business concept to a board to have it voted on, where it may or may not be accepted. We would be out the five grand, the six months, and probably the location by that time because what landlord would want to hold their property for you in sheer hopes that everything would work out?

The city officials and our agent representing us on the deal advised us to let it go and move on. What? Give up? We were so close. NO. I wouldn't accept it. The fire raged within me. How dare they try to make that decision for me. I had people who needed this business. I had a duty to them (it didn't matter they didn't know this yet). I knew it. Everything in my body screamed at me to go down to that city myself and speak to someone in person. The other part of me was trying to convince myself that everyone else was right – that I should just let it go and move on. I couldn't do nothing. I couldn't ignore it. The desire to do this was too strong. So, I went. Not knowing anything about city permits and business codes, I marched myself into the business planning and development department among a sea of contractors, signed in, and waited. When the first city representative told me they loved the idea but it was not possible, I asked to speak to someone else. When they weren't available, I made sure to be back when they were. I kept showing up, I kept calling. I kept speaking to different people. I knew there had to be a way. 'No', to me, just meant 'not that way'. I was too close to let this go now. I kept asking the universe to put me in contact with the person who would help make this happen.

The universe delivered. I was greeted by one of the senior planners in charge at the city. Once again I explained my business concept to him and to my surprise, he said, "Well let's have a closer look and see how we could make this happen." It was true that this business wasn't permitted (because really, it had never existed before) but perhaps if we found something else similar that was, we might be able to get a permit and move forward. That's all I needed to hear.

With this new shred of hope, I was able to access the city's business permit and legislation information on their website, study what they had already accepted in the past, and put together a proposal which I immediately submitted to them. This was my one shot. They had to have a meeting, collectively look at it, discuss it, and vote on it. It took about three weeks of me going in there nearly every day to follow up, and our agent convincing (begging) the property manager to give us more time, until we finally got an answer. When the lady in charge of my case called and said we were "good to go" I had to ask her to repeat herself three times. "So the business is accepted? So it will be allowed in the city? We still have to sign the lease and do construction – will it still be allowed after all that?" I kept asking, fearing that I heard her wrong each time she answered. In one final confirmation she said "Yes, your business is accepted and you are allowed to open" as if it were no big deal, but to me it was everything for which I had been hoping and praying. What was even more amazing – everyone at the city loved our business and couldn't wait for it to open! We had gotten them on our side!

We now had a location, a secured lease, and a business for which the city was excited. Now we had to find a contractor to transform this dark, chopped up, closed off former exercise dance studio, into a light, bright, open-concept puppy palace.

When our first quote came in at $85,000 (not including materials, the furniture I had already purchased, and everything else I was going to need to make the space look beautiful, not to mention to get the business up and running), I felt a huge lump arise in my throat, but quickly shrugged it off. Clearly this guy was just way overpriced. It couldn't cost THAT much. When the next quote came in at over $100,000, all hell broke loose inside of me. I was sick to my stomach. We couldn't spend that! We didn't even *have* that! My mind started to spiral… we had just signed this lease... we were committed for the next four years... we couldn't afford to renovate the space to get the business open... how were we supposed to do this... why didn't we know how expensive these things were... how do other small business owners do this? What were we going to do? How could we have been so naive and irresponsible not to know this?

As I took a deep breath and tried to shake off the feeling of making a horrible gut-wrenching mistake, I heard another voice deep inside saying, "Just keep moving forward. Everyone we're meeting is taking us to where we're supposed to be." Not knowing where to turn next, we called our agent to see if he had any connections with anyone who could help us. He gave us the name of an architect, who came down to meet us at the space. He toured the property, but was leaving to go out of town that night so he made a call right there to someone he thought might be able to do the job. We arranged to meet him the next day.

We walked the entire space with the new contractor explaining our vision, what we wanted to achieve, and why we were so motivated to do what we were doing. We explained what we had been through and how it was my passion to be able to help new owners with their puppies and assist in building that incredible puppy-human bond. He asked us what our budget was. We were brutally honest – and even the amount we said was a stretch for us. It was less than a third of our lowest quote we had received at that point. I thought for sure he was going to laugh hysterically and walk right out. Instead, he looked at us, I could see him really thinking things through for a few minutes, then he said that he absolutely loved what we were doing and he wanted to be a part of this project and help us out. He had five dogs himself at home, and even fostered dogs. He believed in what we were doing and understood how much owners needed this, that he told us he would do our construction for us at our budget price.

Marco and I looked at each other. We were in shock. I think my heart stopped when I fully digested what he was saying. I all but burst into tears of gratitude and relief. This was it, this was our last piece of the puzzle to make this all come together. We had someone who not only believed in my dream, but was now going to physically build its home.

Four months after construction commenced, The Puppy Academy opened its doors for business. Years of planning, visioning, manifesting, encouragement from family and friends, guidance from mentors, and not to mention having to endure a tough puppyhood experience by myself, all carried me to this point now – my dream had finally come to life.

The response has been overwhelmingly wonderful. People are blown away by what we have created: the concept, the need for the services we are providing, and how the space looks and feels. Owners are ecstatic about the results they're seeing in their pups – even after just the first day with us! It's been everything I ever hoped it to be, and it's only getting better.

We get compliments on EVERYTHING: our logo and branding, our website, our team of amazing trainers, our space and the paint colors on the walls, the tiles on the floor... everything! It is so rewarding to see people respond positively to your dream. Every compliment I have received has been reassurance to me that this was the right move – I needed to do this and I'm thankful I listened to that voice.

In every single client we have had the privilege of helping and in every single owner I have been able to meet, I see a part of myself in them. I understand what they're going through, and I know with full confidence how we can help each and every one of them. I am so grateful to be able to provide this incredible service to support them and to help make puppyhood easier in a way no one else has done. It is my full intention to build a puppy empire that helps new puppy owners all over the world by nurturing that special bond and experiencing the unconditional love a puppy can bring.

Through this journey, I have often reflected on how I got here and how all this came together. When I first got Coconut and Marco got stuck out of the country, I thought my life was falling apart. I prayed constantly asking for a sign of why this was happening and what I should be doing. I was desperate for guidance. I didn't realize until much later, it was during this time that things were not falling apart; they were actually all starting to come together for me.

I can't believe how worried I used to be about figuring out my destiny. The sleepless nights and countless hours lost from being consumed over the pressure of carefully choosing what I might want to do with the rest of my life. It sounds so silly to me now because I've realized that we really don't choose our destiny. Our **destiny** chooses us. It can – and probably will – show up when and how you least expect it. It's up to us to listen, then act.

My greatest advice would be when you hear that inner voice speak to you and you feel that fire burning inside you about it – don't ignore it. Don't talk yourself out of it. Build that image of it even more in your mind and go for it. If you can see it, if you believe it, and if you are committed to it, the universe will work in unimaginable ways to deliver it to you. Even if it's through a mischievous little puppy you never thought you'd have.

ABOUT RICCI & MARCO

Ricci Reardin Mills and Marco Mills have been avid studiers of universal law for the last several years and have accredited their success to their dedication to personal development through working with incredible mentors like Peggy McColl, Sandy Gallagher and Bob Proctor. Both from Toronto, Canada, Ricci and Marco now enjoy building their multiple businesses while living by the beach in Southern California, with their pup Coconut.

DISCOVERING YOUR TRUE WORLD

By Trisha Leconte

Why is it that when we are born, we can see ourselves as anything we want to be, do, or have, but somewhere along the way we start limiting ourselves? We come up with all these excuses embedding false beliefs into our minds. We create a concept of reality which is not reality and one which is influenced by other people and our past. Most of the time, we don't like or aren't happy with it because the perception of our world is an unhappy one where we keep having to settle in life.

I was a software engineer for almost 10 years and since I went to college for computer engineering and earned my Master's in software engineering, I figured I would retire as a software engineer. I mean, that's what most people do; they remain in the same career until they retire. Les Brown said, "Most people fail in life, not because they aim too high and miss. Most people fail in life because they aim too low and hit."

Looking back, that's exactly what I did. I aimed too low. My only goal after graduating college was to find any computer engineering job, and once I did, I thought I was set. I thought I didn't need to strive to do anything anymore. I mean, becoming a software engineer is a great achievement and it's also a respectable profession, isn't it? This was the reality of my world.

Unfortunately, it took something tragic in my life to occur for me to snap out of it and realize there was more for me in life than receiving a paycheck every two weeks. As I began to understand my true potential, I started making big changes. I believe that everyone has a divine mission and purpose in life. It starts with redefining your world – the world of false beliefs and limiting ideas.

I came to the conclusion we have unlimited potential through discovering worlds – discovering there was much more out there than I ever imagined and that there are more successful ways to do things than we were taught. Do you remember the story of Jack and the Beanstalk? Jack found these magic beans. He planted them, and they grew to be a huge, tall beanstalk into the clouds. When Jack climbed up, he discovered a whole new world that he never knew existed.

We all have unlimited potential. We all have magic beans inside us. All we have to do is plant and nourish them. My favorite quote by Steve Bow says, "God's gift to you is more talent and ability than you can possibly use in this lifetime. Your gift to God is to develop as much of that talent and ability as you can in this lifetime."

Like I mentioned earlier, it sometimes takes a tragic event in life to shift you on to a new path, and that's how it started for me.

World #1: The start of my transformation

On May 10, 2010, I was enjoying a fun team event at my job when the phone rang. It was my mom which I found strange because she doesn't call me during work. I answered the phone but wasn't prepared to hear what she told me: my dad's cancer had returned. I tried to contain myself as I headed to the bathroom. Thoughts flooded my mind: my dad's going to do chemo again, he's going to suffer again, what will happen to him now, why didn't the treatment work after all? I couldn't take it anymore, with my back pressed against the bathroom stall, I slid down and started to cry. I did not want my dad to suffer.

My sister and I became health conscious ever since we started excelling in high school track and field. Knowing that healthy foods were important, we decided to give up fast food, candy, and soda. In fact, all we drank was water. With our dad's health on the line, my sister and I knew we had to do something. We had to cure our dad since chemo and radiation obviously did not work.

We didn't even know if cancer was curable at the time, we simply knew we had to do something. We bought a juicer and started juicing vegetables.

Bless my dad's heart, he scarfed down anything we gave him without hesitation: broccoli, kale, wheat grass, cabbage, watercress, bell pepper. No matter what the concoction smelled or tasted like, he drank it with a smile.

Magic happens when you take action towards a big goal, especially when you have no idea how to accomplish it. I attracted into my life my chiropractor's mother; she was a health coach who worked with cancer patients. I hired her for my dad... and for myself. This was where I discovered this new world of health.

I didn't know you could heal the body of anything using natural foods, herbs and supplements. I found it very disturbing this information was never taught to the public. Instead, we rely on doctors to prescribe us medication. I remember going to the doctor for help only to be told, "We're not sure what you have." By changing my diet, I cured my chronic cough, cramps, acne and became much healthier. Fascinated by this discovery, I decided to become a certified health coach. I wasted no time in spreading the word and in helping people discover this new found world.

In the end, my dad passed away from complications in 2014 due to all the chemo and radiation. I miss him every day and I will never forget he gave me my greatest gift – finding my destiny.

My hunger for learning more about this new world kept expanding and I was determined to discover what else was not being taught in society.

World #2: The strangest secret in the world

After being certified as a health coach, I had one thing on my mind – success. How would I become successful? One of the first books I came across was called *The Miracle Morning*, by Hal Elrod. In his book, he suggested that simply waking up early to practice some disciplined principles, used by other successful people, we can get a lot done. These disciplined principles included: journaling, exercising, meditating, reading, repeating affirmations, and visualizing. I remember wondering to myself how was I going to wake up early enough to get these done? I was already waking up at 6a.m. to get to work by 7a.m. For me, this was considered early. Waking up at 5am seemed too darn early, I mean, it was pitch dark outside and cold at that time. Despite my initial reservations, I was determined to do it so I developed a plan.

Day 1, the alarm goes off. I get up immediately, excited to start. Day 2, alarm goes off. Groaning, I tell myself it's too early, and I go back to bed. Day 3, 4, 5, and on, the alarm goes off. Again, I tell myself it's too early, it's too dark outside, and it's too cold to get up. Week 2 was a little better, even though I snoozed the alarm for as long as I could. Week 3 was about the same. Clearly this was not working out how I wanted – I needed a new plan. I decided to put a timer on the bright lights in my room and on my bedroom heater. The next day, my room was toasty, but all I did was pull the covers over my head and went back to sleep. It was only a month later when I decided to move my alarm clock across the room did I begin waking up at 5a.m. Finally, I was getting a lot done! I was on a roll.

This was the first time a book made such a difference in my life. What else could I learn? Little did I know the secret of the ages is locked up in books. After setting a goal of reading one book a week, I wasted no time in getting started. I read books from some of most successful experts in the field of personal development which included Jim Rohn, Wayne Dyer, Marianne Williamson, Napoleon Hill, Neville Goddard, Eckhart Tolle, and many more.

It was then I came across Earl Nightingale's *The Strangest Secret*. Things in my life really clicked after I read where he said, "We become what we think about." Of course! How did I not know this before? It made perfect sense. Again, I felt like I discovered another new world which few people knew about. I started learning more about the power of the mind.

It wasn't that long ago where I thought 5a.m. was too early because it was dark outside; but who said the sun must be up before it's time to get out of bed? It wasn't that long ago where I thought I had to be a software engineer for the rest of my life because it's the degree I held. It also wasn't that long ago where I thought I had to move to Texas to buy a house because I couldn't afford one in Silicon Valley.

My thoughts were holding me back. They were forcing me to settle in life instead of creating the life I wanted. If I change my thoughts, my entire world would change? Yes, and this is exactly what happened. Although it was hard because my dad was still struggling with cancer, I knew I could not hold on to the anger, fear, and sadness any longer. Whenever I felt these feelings building up inside me, I changed my thoughts, until, eventually, I became known as "the most positive person" among my family and friends.

My new attitude in life improved my life in many areas. I was happier and more loving. I was enjoying my job and socializing more. Life kept getting better and better.

I learned from training to be a health coach that the more good you put into your body, the less bad you put in. I decided to take this approach with my thoughts and that's when I discovered world #3.

World #3: Unlimited Potential

One day, while watching YouTube videos I came across a motivational one with Les Brown. Immediately, I was attracted to his voice and the way he spoke. I thought to myself, "It would be so cool to be able to speak like this when doing my Toastmasters speeches." I decided to study him, and after watching a few of his videos, I realized how much I absolutely loved his messages. Captivated by his inspirational messages, I created a playlist of every one of his motivational videos I could find.

At work, at the gym, and even in the shower, I played the motivational videos over and over again. In the morning, before bed, and even just wandering the house, the playlist was on repeat. I couldn't get enough. "You have greatness within you," was one of Les Brown's popular sayings. I became so familiar with his words that I found myself reciting them aloud with all the passion and conviction, as he had done. People passing me in the car probably thought I was crazy; my husband definitely thought I was crazy, and my mom and sister thought I had gone off the deep end. To me, that was ok because it meant I was on the right track. I was breaking away from the 'norm'.

I realized that I stopped watching TV, stopped listening to the radio, and even stopped watching Hulu at work… shhhhhh… please keep this our little secret. Instead, many hours of my day was spent listening to motivational and inspirational content. I had cut out the trash and replaced it with priceless, golden material. Over and over, through repetition, the words, ideas, and emotions were seeping into my mind. I really did have greatness in me! My dreams and desires were possible. "You got to be hunnnngry," says Les Brown, and that's exactly what I was.

I love YouTube. Through the related videos list, I found other inspiring people with amazing content such as Eric Thomas, TD Jakes, Tony Robins, Walter Bond… and then I came across a video from Bob Proctor. All his ideas resonated with me. I finally understood I had unlimited potential after listening for many hours to what all these people were saying. I could be, do, and have anything I wanted. But what did I want?

In April 2016, I figured it all out. I decided I needed to see Bob Proctor and learn more from him. After attending one of his events called the Matrixx, it became clear to me what I wanted in life. I had discovered my destiny. I wanted to become a top motivational speaker and life coach, and I knew the key to my success would be my thoughts. I told myself that just because I'm shy and introverted doesn't mean I cannot be a top motivational speaker. I also reasoned with myself that simply because I have never run a business doesn't mean I can't be successful. In even more striking words, I told myself that just because I am a software engineer doesn't mean I can't do something else.

It was time for this diamond to shine! I decided to take back control of my life and do what I wanted to do. As you probably guessed my family, friends, and even co-workers were completely shocked when I shared with them my plans.

On August 12, 2016, I retired from software engineering to start my own business – helping other people discover this amazing information I have learned, to take back control of their lives, and show them how to get anything they want. I decided to work with Bob Proctor as one of his consultants.

This is only the beginning for me and the future looks bright. Why? Because I'm in control of my life and I can do, be, and have anything I want. I know that I am living my dreams today because of the love for my dad, which during hard times allowed me to discover a hidden world. That's the way it happens sometimes, your life changes due to a tragic event, but it doesn't have to be that way for you.

What you must understand is we already have everything we need inside us. We do not need to go in search of anything. I love using the analogy of a glass window. If you take a new glass window and hold it to the light, it will shine through perfectly. The window is perfect. If you do not care for the window, over time, it will start to get cloudy and develop a layer of film over it. The light will not shine through it as brightly as it did before but it is still a perfect glass window – it just needs to be cleaned. The same thing applies to us. We are all perfect and have this wonderful light inside of us; however, after years of developing these false ideas and beliefs about ourselves and the world around us, our window becomes cloudy preventing our true light from shining through.

Plant the magic beans you have inside of you and by taking action towards your dream, you will discover worlds you have never known before – you will discover your **destiny**.

ABOUT TRISHA

Trisha Leconte is a PGI consultant from California, dedicated to helping people recognize their unlimited potential and get the results they want in life. She was a software engineer for about 10 years before she realized her true potential and decided to take a new path to help and inspire people. Understanding the power of the mind, she quit her job and started working with Bob Proctor. She is now a PGI consultant, working with people to make their goals and dreams come true, while doing the same for herself. The key to life is Keep Evolving Yourself.

About the Authors

More information about all the authors can be found at:
http://www.peggymccoll.com.

**Visit
http://www.peggymccoll.com.**

for more information about this book
and all of Peggy's other books and programs available.

We make your literary wish come true

The authors of *Destinies*

have partnered with

The Literary Fairies

who have a mission to give to those who have experienced an adversity or disability an opportunity to become a published author while sharing a story to uplift, inspire and entertain the world.

Visit www.theliteraryfairies.com to find out how YOU could become a published author or where you can help grant a literary wish.

More details provided at
www.theliteraryfairies.com